PRAISE FOR
THE ACCIDENTAL APHORIST

"There's a poet and essayist on the scene whom I love, named Phil Cousineau. Witness the blazing sincerity of his *Once and Future Myths*. Also, his deeply helpful *Beyond Forgiveness*. Once again in his new book he proves his deftness with words and images. His gift reminds me of my distant relative, T. S. Eliot, and his penchant for the aphoristic phrase. Long may Cousineau weave his mosaicist word magic."
> —Alexander Eliot, author of *Three Hundred Years of American Painting, Sight and Outsight* and *Because it was Beautiful*

"Phil Cousineau's aphorisms will delight, amuse, provoke and astonish, demonstrating how much wit and wisdom can be mined from a lifelong practice of listening and observing. These pages read like a series of literary fortune cookies, made with a dash of Montaigne, Dorothy Parker, James Joyce, and Lao-Tzu. Use this book as an oracle. Or keep it by your bed as for those restless nights when you need to restore your own unbearable lightness of being."
> —Valerie Andrews, author of *The Secret Lives of Ordinary Things*, and *A Passion for this Earth*.

"*The Accidental Aphorist* is another wonderful Phil Cousineau metaphor for the way that we come to wisdom, in short bursts of imagination. Readers will be quoting from this marvelous collection for years to come, and be inspired by his passion and commitment to the deep art of writing."

     —Angeles Arrien, author of *The Four-Fold Way* and *The Nine Muses*

"A wise saying is not an aphorism until it is lived. Phil Cousineau's remarkable collection comes from just such a lived life and I relished my reading of them."

     —Robert A. Johnson, author of *He, She, We,* and *Balancing Heaven and Earth*

"I resort to the Prince de Ligne's method and withdraw from your brilliant gems, your nimble wit, into solitude where they sparkle in the dark."

     —James Norwood Pratt, award-winning author of
       The Tea Lover's Treasury and
       The Wine Bibber's Bible

For Eileen,
in thanks for
helping mom my
aphorisms
through
the world!

THE
ACCIDENTAL
APHORIST

2017

BOOKS BY THE AUTHOR

The Hero's Journey: Joseph Campbell on his Life and Work, 1990

Deadlines: A Rhapsody on a Theme of Famous Last Words, 1991

The Soul of the World: A Modern Book of Hours (with Eric Lawton), 1993

Riders on the Storm: My Life with Jim Morrison and The Doors (by John Densmore with Phil Cousineau), 1993

Soul: An Archaeology: Readings from Socrates to Ray Charles, 1994

Prayers at 3 a.m.: Poems for the Middle of the Night, 1995

UFOs: A Mythic Manual for the Millennium, 1995

Design Outlaws: The Frontier of the 21st Century (with Christopher Zelov), 1996

Soul Moments: Marvelous Stories of Synchronicity, 1997

The Art of Pilgrimage: A Seeker's Guide to Making Travel Sacred, 1998

Riddle Me This: A World Treasury of Folk and Literary Puzzles, 1999

The Soul Aflame: A Modern Book of Hours (with Eric Lawton), 2000

The Book of Roads: Travel Stories from Michigan to Marrakesh, 2000

Once and Future Myths: The Power of Ancient Stories, 2001

The Way Things Are: Conversations with Huston Smith on the Spiritual Life, 2003

The Olympic Odyssey: Rekindling the Spirit of the Great
    Games, 2004
The Blue Museum: Poems, 2004
A Seat at the Table: The Struggle for American Indian
    Religious Freedom, 2005
Angkor Wat: The Marvelous Enigma (photographs), 2006
Night Train: New Poems, 2007
The Jaguar People: An Amazonian Chronicle
    (photographs), 2007
Stoking the Creative Fires: 9 Ways to Rekindle
    Imagination, 2008
Fungoes and Fastballs: Great Moments in Baseball
    Haiku, 2008
The Meaning of Tea (with Scott Chamberlin Hoyt), 2009
City 21: The Search for the Second Enlightenment in the
    Urban World (with Chris Zelov), 2009
The Oldest Story in the World: Meditations on
    Storytelling, 2010
The Song of the Open Road (photographs), 2010
Wordcatcher: An Odyssey into the World of Wonderful
    Words, 2010
Beyond Forgiveness: Reflections on Atonement, 2010
The Art of Travel Journal, 2011
Around the World in Eighty Faces (photographs), 2011
And Live Rejoicing: Chapters from a Charmed Life (by
    Huston Smith with Phil Cousineau), 2012
The Painted Word: A Treasure Chest of Remarkable
    Words, 2012
Shadowcatcher (photographs), 2012

Burning the Midnight Oil: Illuminating Words for the
   Long Night's Journey into Night, 2013
The Soul and Spirit of Tea (with Scott Chamberlin
   Hoyt), 2013
Crepuscular: New Photographs, 2014
The Book of Roads: Travel Stories (New and Expanded
   Edition), 2015
Rasa: A Pilgrimage to India (photographs), 2015
Fungoes & Fastballs: New and Expanded Edition, 2016
The Accidental Aphorist: A Curiosity Cabinet of
   Aphorisms, Maxims, Pochades and Pensées, Gnomic
   Observations ... and Afterthoughts, 2016
Who Stole the Arms of the Venus de Milo?
   [forthcoming]
Waiting for Kaline: A Baseball Fable for All Ages
   (by Phil Cousineau and Jack Cousineau)
   [forthcoming]
The Lost Notebooks of Sisyphus [forthcoming]

AUDIO BOOKS

The Art of Pilgrimage: A Seeker's Guide to Making Travel Sacred, 1998

Once and Future Myths: The Power of Ancient Stories, 2001

A Seat at the Table: The Struggle for American Indian Religious Freedom, 2005

Beyond Forgiveness: Reflections on Atonement, 2009

Wordcatcher: An Odyssey into the World of Wonderful Words, 2010

The Painted Word: A Treasure Chest of Remarkable Words, 2012

Burning the Midnight Oil: Illuminating Words for the Long Night's Journey into Day, 2014

The Book of Roads: A Life Made of Travel, 2015

THE ACCIDENTAL APHORIST: A Curiosity Cabinet of
Aphorisms, Maxims, Epigrams, Pochades and Pensées, Gnomic
Observations, Laconics and Lucubrations, Backthoughts and
Afterthoughts

Published in a limited edition by Sisyphus Press
P.O. Box 330098 San Francisco, California 94133
To reorder please contact us at: www.philcousineau.net

Library of Congress Control Number (LCCN)

ISBN: 978-0-9835920-9-9

Grateful acknowledgement to Michael and Jeanne Adams for the
kind use of their Guest House in Carmel Highlands, where this
book was first given shape and color; thanks, too, to the
proprietors of Renvyle House, in Connemara, Ireland, where a
second draft commenced, and to the Hydroussa Hotel, on Hydra,
in the Greek islands, for a sabbatical in the fall of 2016, where
this book was completed.

Cover photograph: Ruins of Library of Pergamum, 3rd century,
Pergamum, Turkey, 2015. Photograph by Phil Cousineau.

Cover and book design by Jim Shubin, BookAlchemist.net

The Accidental Aphorist is typeset in American Typewriter, Sabon

Frontispiece photograph:
"Columns," Temple of Bassae, Greece, 2014.

Back cover: Author Photo by Jo Beaton Cousineau, 2016.

First edition.
First printing: February 2017
10 9 8 7 6 5 4 3 2 1

To three true boon companions,

James Norwood Pratt,
with thanks for the Fellowship of Tea Leaves

and

Mikkel Aaland,
with gratitude for the Friends of the Sauna

and

Anthony Lawlor
with a bow to the Fraternity of Pilgrims

CONTEMPLATING THE COLUMNS
THE TEMPLE OF BASSAE, GREECE, 2014
PHOTOGRAPHY BY PHIL COUSINEAU

THE ACCIDENTAL APHORIST

Phil Cousineau
with photographs by the author

A Curiosity Cabinet of
Aphorisms,
Maxims, Epigrams,
Pochades and Pensées,
Gnomic Observations,
Laconic Lucubrations,
Fragments from the Notebooks,
Back Thoughts and
Afterthoughts

SISYPHUS PRESS

"Aphorisms representing a knowledge broken
do invite men to inquire further."
—Francis Bacon, 1561–1626

"The only way to read a book of aphorisms without being
bored is to open it at random and, having
found something that interests you, close
the book and meditate."
—Prince De Ligne, *Mes ecarts*, 1796

"Tell the truth but tell it slant—

...

The truth must dazzle slowly,
Or every man go blind—"
—Emily Dickinson, 1830–1886

"To find my home in one sentence, concise,
as if hammered in metal. Not to enchant anybody.
Not to earn a lasting name in posterity."
—Czeslaw Milosz, 1980

IN LIEU OF A PREFACE

Strange times call for curious books, fractured times for fragmented ones. Written in the spirit of the venerable cabinet of curiosities, I have salvaged here a few of the most meaningful scritches and scratches from forty-plus years of my own notebooks, marvels from my travel journals, and oddments from my research on a plethora of subjects. Behind the cabinet doors can be found the ephemera from years of workshops, art and literary tours, and interviews. There are also scraps rescued from old air-line tickets, gum wrappers, ripped envelopes, beer-stained bar coasters, and even the backs of old baseball cards.

As Billie Holliday moaned, "One never knows, does one?" You never know when a single word or phrase will come along and spark a fresh idea, make an exciting connection, even forge a bold new work.

The Accidental Aphorist reveals the tenacity of Lady Day's bluesy question, with a twist and a turn here and there, to reflect the doubt that has alternately inspired and tormented me since I was a callow teenager writing for my hometown newspaper, the Wayne Dispatch, outside Detroit: After all your learning and all your adventures, *What do you really know?*

The sayings here represent the spirit at the heart of my peripatetic life ever since, an insistence on posing questions rather than demanding answers. The range, then, is wildly eclectic, from the writing life to mythology, art to philosophy, travel to sports.

As arbitrary as the selections may appear, a pattern slowly emerges, or at least a *persistence of vision*, as filmmakers say. The prismatic phrase describes the optical illusion created by a series of discrete images merging into a single image in the mind—what my friend, the culture historian Theodore Roszak, called the *flicker*—that creates the perception of motion.

Likewise, moving through these pages is the flickering image of one man's relentless self-examination and ceaseless observing of the world, held together by a slender black thread of skepticism that, ironically, keeps it altogether. And so the sayings gathered here are indeed fragments from the notebooks, splinters from my travel journals, rather than phrases burnished to a fare-thee-well. They reveal not the ideal but the labyrinthine ways of one man's mind as he tried to overcome the fear of never being concise enough, and the dread that my perception of reality has never been as clear as I thought it was.

Moreover, there is something beyond the impulse to make sense of the obsessive note taking and unabashed quote mongering that marks this work. Something more practical inspired me to assemble this collection. For years I have been asked if I harbored any secrets about how to lead a prolific life, which I have taken to mean an ardent desire to forge a path of *constant* creativity. "It's no secret" has been the usual wry response, followed by a heartfelt remark, *If you don't love the work, it won't work*. Well, love and work, plus reflection and play, endurance and passion. However, I warn, these qualities amount to nothing, if we don't develop a daily practice. As I heard legendary basketball John Wooden once say, "If you don't have time to do it *right*, when you will ever have time to do it over?"

That said, nearly every day over the last few decades, I have followed two daily such practices designed to spark my creative fires. Every morning I routinely open one or more of my notebooks in search of a word or phrase or image that might stir the cauldron of my imagination, as well as exercise the muscles of memory. Every afternoon or evening, in the spirit of bibliomancy —the venerable tradition of divination through books— I pull a book off the bulging shelves of my personal library. Closing my eyes, I open it and choose a passage at random, trusting now in the gods of serendipity. Whether it's the edition of Montaigne's Essays that I inherited from my father, the *Collected Poems* of Emily Dickinson, or a grin-inducing volume of Yogi Berra's unwitting witticisms, I read a passage or three, then reread it until I've learned it by heart. Over the course of the day I mull over the words until they surrender some relevance or meaning to me, not just because they have been barnacled with reputation by being included in this or that anthology of ennobling quotations. Or I ponder them until I've absorbed the author's rhythms and cadences the way a painter might visit the work his favorite artist in a museum in hopes of some cosmic osmosis from the work of the masters.

Thus emboldened or just plain driven by untold demons—or *daemons*—I plunge into whatever writing project I am currently engrossed in, and write, for better or for worse, till the plume drops from my hand, or the inkwell runs dry in my scriptorium. Figuratively speaking, of course, since I only write my first drafts by hand. The rest is fated to come from the ghost in the machine, the soul of my electronic keyboard.

Together, these deceptively simple daily practices have been my way of taking to heart Emerson's timeless advice about creativity being the capacity to stoke your own fire—rather than waiting for the muses to magically infuse you with inspiration. The movement from creative *theory* to creative *work* makes this more than a collection of written or spoken words. Rather than this being the result of compulsive list making, it is a gathering of words I've tried to live by, which is an ink of a different color. An inkling of a more articulate life. Virtually every one of the lines, stories, verses or anecdotes, has jumped off the page of my notebooks and journals, then sparked, flared, and caught fire as a poem, short story, essay, script, review, or full-length book. Moreover, scores of these lines have been used to spark or prompt my students in the classes I've taught since 1981 on a wide range of subjects from mythology and art to literature and travel, even the history of sports.

Strange to say, it is embarrassing for a *philobiblion*, or book lover, as my Greek friends have anointed me, to admit to an embarrassing omission in my *remembery*, as opposed to my *forgettery*. Despite my lifelong passion for words it never occurred to me that there was a name for what people like me are wont to do, which is collect and repeat the wisest things ever said on record, and occasionally coining our own aphorisms.

That word would be *aphorist*.

Unfortunately, *aphorist* sounds far more hifalutin than what it really is, which tends to be more *lofalutin*, to coin a much-needed word. For me, an aphorist is anyone who is concise and pithy in their writing or speaking. More than a wag and less than a gasbag, an aphorist loves words enough to care about the luxuriousness of language and the dexterity of phrasing. But a true aphorist is more philosophical than clever, which is the realm of the epigram; more startling then platitudinous, which veers towards the proverb or the maxim. An agile aphorist gets a word in edgewise by making their words edgy, wise by virtue of their edginess. Their sayings are so personal and memorable they are inimitable. No one sounds quite like Michel de Montaigne or Groucho Marx or Mae West. That is why we quote them and elicit laughter or gasps of wonder, often just at the drop of their name.

The deft aphorist, or phraseologist, if you will, appears to say things better than we possibly can, or the way we like to think we would if we were more clever or fluent. But I'm fascinated with another aspect, the artesian depths of the beautifully said. How is it, I wonder, that the most quotable writers and thinkers of all time have the uncanny capacity to say what we have been recently thinking, as if they have been reading our mind? How on earth is this possible?

Consider the stunned admission of the critic Bernard Levin, writing of Montaigne, the pioneer of the personal essay, "How could he have known all that about me?" The brilliant German novelist Stefan Zweig described the impact of the same *Essays* even more elliptically, "Here is a 'you' in which my 'I' is reflected."

Therein lies the great paradox. We who love language often learn how to think for ourselves by quoting others. Ideally, we do so in hopes of training ourselves how to say or write something worthwhile, even original, in our own unmistakable voice.

Of course, there is a twist, as there always is with aphoristic writing. Rather than *aiming* to be profound—a velvet verbal trap for writers, teachers, and conversationalists alike—aphorisms seem to *happen* to the writer or speaker. Classic sayings—such as those of Goethe, Nietzsche, Emerson, Fields, Parker or Le Guin—feel like solar flares of sudden wit or wisdom that are paradoxically both timeless and spontaneous.

Contrariwise, to set out to write wisely usually looks forced, like trying to see better by squinting, or singing better by screeching. Since the musings of Socrates in Athens' agora, the wisest sayings tend to come from those who don't know or even care that they might be privy to important insights. Often it isn't until much later that their listeners and later their readers recognized a *frisson* of truth that was both intensely personal and mysteriously universal.

Extemporized or predigested, I've come to think of the aphorism as anti-snark, an antidote for cynicism. *Snark* is one of those rare words that *sounds* exactly as it means. Originating in Lewis Carroll's corrosively humorous poem *The Hunting of the Snark*, the sonicky word is a combination of *sneer* and *snort*. With one swipe of his pen, the Oxford don described an elusive and menacing creature that has proved immortal.

"For the snark was Boojum, you see," reads the strange last line of the poem, and a scarifying thought it was to the readers of the day—and ours. For what Carroll revealed was the snark's terrifying ability to make its victims "suddenly vanish away." The snark lives on—or *squirms* on—in our use of the word today to express a sneer you can hang a side of beef from, the snorting comment that cuts its victim deep enough to make them want to vanish, disappear, wish they were never born.

Consider the stiletto-sharp contrast between the aphorism and the snarkism, which cuts to the heart of this book. The former has a transformative power to make you *appear* to yourself, in the sense that reading or hearing or writing a bona fide aphorism allows you to suddenly recognize your own innermost thoughts. Conversely, the latter has the transmogrifying power of making you *disappear*, the result of the incredible shrinking power of the withering remark.

Since the time of the rapscallion author La Rochefoucauld and his collection of *Maximes* there has been a general agreement that aphorisms are distinct because they feature a subversive streak. The ones that are passed down from generation to generation tend to feature a whiplash ending, a jack-in-the-box surprise, a verbal sleight-of-hand. Ironically, as essayist John Gross points out, it is often the tendency of the maxim to blithely generalize that aphorisms aim to subvert by condensing and compressing, abbreviating and parenthesizing. Neither does the aphorism symbolize— but it does *aphorize*.

Who can improve on Virginia Woolf's deservedly famous line, "A woman must have money and a room of her own if she is to write fiction"? "Nothing great has great beginnings," Joseph Le Maistre's headscratching saying, cannot be said any better. Nor can Stanislaw Jerzy Lec's quirky observation "It is unhealthy to live.

He who lives, dies." Then there's Lillian Hellman's agitating notion, "Life starts out as hopes, and ends up as habits."

To honor the vigorous variety of aphoristic writing, I have interleaved through my own sayings a few epigrams, adages, maxims, *pensées*, and axioms from their most deft practitioners. The coruscating passages of Cyrano de Bergerac (via Edmond Rostand), Joseph Joubert, Emerson, Ambrose Bierce, Sappho, Virginia Woolf, Joyce Carol Oates, Oscar Wilde, Mae West, Susan Sontag and Woody Allen do more than sparkle. Their inclusion is a doff of my old blue fedora to those pens and minds from whom I've learned so much. They and so many more taught me how much time and thought is required to write so little but so well, which is a rhapsody on the theme of reading to ignite a firestorm of creative writing. To honor these agile aphorists reminds us that often we only require a quiet squeezing of the bellows over the ashes of our creative fires, only need a glow rather than a roar.

So allow me, if you will, to suggest a couple of ways for you to approach this book. Read it cover to cover, if the spirit moves you, pausing over the passages that speak to you. If nothing immediately leaps off the page, try again later. If and when one talks to you, consider it then reconsider it, brood over it until it cracks open and comes to life. There in the crack, as Leonard Cohen wrote aphoristically, is where the light gets in; it is also where we find the *broken knowledge* that Francis Bacon believed was the source of our most haunted aphorisms.

If you are feeling frisky, try to approach the book more randomly. Riffle through the pages. Poke around until you find a passage that moves like quicksilver through your mind. Put your reading faith in the gods of serendipity and synchronicity. Since the time of Heraclitus there has been not an opposing but complementary practice of long contemplation, and that is the art of the *quick glance*—an ardent belief that there is never any one final understanding of anything.

Or as Yogi put it, "There are deep depths there."

However you stride into these pages, imagine, if you will, how the Swiss artist and visionary Paul Klee defined his method in his personal notebooks. "A drawing is simply taking a line out for a walk." For many years, his deft description has inspired my own way of thinking about reading and writing, and in turn has influenced me to be more playful with my students and more accepting of the essential absurdity of creativity.

With those lines in mind, if you find that one of my aphorisms, notebook musings, a palm-sized story stirs you, or a life-sized parable provokes you, take it out for a walk. See where it leads. Trust the meanders, turn around if you hit a dead end and keep moving, keep reading, and keep the faith. Who knows, a single line might grow into a story, perhaps a poem, maybe a song, even a letter, ideally a conversation.

If the spirit moves you, be bold, be playful, be memorable. Go out and write one of your own.

Phil Cousineau
San Francisco-Paris-Hydra,
September 2009–December 2016

MICHEL DE MONTAIGNE, BY PAUL LANDOWSKI
PARIS, FRANCE, 2009
PHOTOGRAPHY BY PHIL COUSINEAU

The Curiosity Cabinet
Of
Aphorisms

The book was the first time machine.

—⟋⟍—

Every word is a pilgrim, every sentence a sojourn.

—⟋⟍—

The more burnished the satchel the more stories it carries.

—⟋⟍—

I don't know what I believe until I read what I *need* to say.

—⟋⟍—

All I needed to be a writer happened by the time I was twelve. That's astonishing and terrifying at the same time.

—⟋⟍—

Not your faith, but your curiosity is the most holy thing about you.

—⟋⟍—

I think that the forty-hour week is such a brilliant idea, I do it twice a week.

—⟋⟍—

If I want to understand what's happening now, I read an old book; if I want know what's going to happen next, I read an older one.

—⟋⟍⟍—

Word to the wise, as my Grandma Dora used to say. Live so that you wouldn't be afraid to sell the family parrot to the town gossip.

—⟋⟍⟍—

When it suits me I use my quotehanger to hold up my favorite lines so they don't wrinkle.

—⟋⟍⟍—

When my father bought me *The Unabridged Random House Dictionary* for my twelfth birthday I thought it was a book of poems, riddles, jokes, and parables. It was, it is, it will be.

—⟋⟍⟍—

My secret dread is that what I have to say for myself will never be enough—or worse, as wrong as the weird green-skied day when I was a boy and it rained frogs. Not cats and dogs, *frogs*.

—⟋⟍⟍—

Slamming the brakes on your creative life leaves skidmarks on your soul.

I disappear between the bindings of my books, like the Tang Dynasty painter Wu Tao-Tzu, who vanished after creating a wall mural for Emperor Xuanzong. The legend goes that the painting was a glorious landscape teeming with emerald green flora and fauna, a silvery waterfall, and a gaping cave at the foot of a mist-shrouded mountain. When Wu Tao-Tzu unveiled his work, he clapped his hands three times—and stepped right into the painting, passing through a bright red gate, which led to the cave. Smiling, it is said in the annals, Wu Tao-Tzu turned and invited the emperor to join him. Legend has it that the emperor leaned forward, longing to follow, but before he could take a step toward the painting the gate clanked shut, Wu Tao-Tzu turned away and stepped into the cave. Then the painting itself dissolved and disappeared. Every time I lose myself in a mystifying work of art, a song or a story, I too lean forward. And then I disappear where no one can find me.

—〰—

A writer is a person trapped inside a typewriter who can barely reach the keys.

—〰—

Chance does not favor the unprepared mind.

—〰—

The more I think about it, the pen is to the mind what the gnomon is to the sundial. The shadow, not the sun, tells the time, and the truth.

5

When in doubt, live, then read, now write.

— ⟋⟍ —

You can be connected to everyone, everywhere, and still be out of touch.

— ⟋⟍ —

My father turns down the Falcon's car radio, crooks his left arm across the top of the steering wheel and throws his right arm along the top ridge of the continuous faux leather front seat. He runs his hand across the blond stubble of my summer crew cut. Takes a deep breath of the burning leaves in the Civil War-era town cemetery we are passing. Clears his throat. Casts a thousand-mile stare down the long stretch of Michigan Avenue. I follow his gaze into the far, far away and hear the first words of something he feels he needs to tell me: "This used to be called The Old Sauk Trail, which began as a deer path, which makes this one of the oldest roads in the country." My father. Revving up. To tell a story.

— ⟋⟍ —

Startled by the shrill will of the alarm clock this morning, it dawned on me that all advice comes down to this: *Wake up!*

— ⟋⟍ —

A bookstore is the best school.

— ⟋⟍ —

Memory, n. The longer the reach, the stranger the emotion. The remembery is the card you need to get out of the forgettery.

—ɲɲ—

Write your own books and the effort will warm you twice.

—ɲɲ—

Chance. If an artist or writer or scientist—anyone— doesn't mention its role in their work, I'm suspicious. Chances are they're hiding something. That's why they call it blind.

—ɲɲ—

From the travel journals: Perigueux, France, May 1985. On a pilgrimage in the footsteps of my ancestors. I read on the menu of a local café that their favorite son here, the philosopher Michel de Montaigne, asked, *"Que sais-je?"* "What do I know?" Knowing the philosopher painted it along with several other sayings from his famous book of *Essays* onto one of the wooden beams of his library, along with dozens of maxims by his favorite thinkers, moves me in ways I have yet to fathom. Three hundred years later, prodded by his relentless seeking, every day, every night, I ask myself, "What do I know, what do I *really* know?" *Rien, rien, pas encore, pas encore,* comes the noctivagating answer on the dark breath of night. *Pas assez.* Not enough, never enough.

The shortest distance between two people is a story.
Two hundred million, too.

—ẁ—

Insights will befall you, she warned me.

—ẁ—

You know your work is done when you can look at it
and say to yourself: *This is who I am right now. I can
live with this. So let it go—*

—ẁ—

The desire line. The path worn in the ground when the
sidewalk is too straight, too boring, too unnatural.
The desire line. Curving, meandering, swervy. Defiant.
Reflecting the refusal to follow another's path, just our
own feel for the land. Like the way lovers move toward
each other. Never in a straight line, always in meanders.
The sensuous moving sinuously. Out of desire.

—ẁ—

Don't think, work, then think, then work again. Think
again, if you're not working.

—ẁ—

To seek the stories that matter and care about them
more than truth takes us halfway to where it matters.

A love poem is a caress with words.

—⁓—

Do you want to know a secret? Lean in. I have never told this to anyone. Everything I have written explores what I found trapped inside a piece of amber I picked up on a beach long ago. So long ago I can't remember if I did or not, and if I did, where I left it.

—⁓—

We can't will who we love, we can only love as we will.

—⁓—

Overheard outside City Lights Bookstore, San Francisco, April 1996. Nervous young couple. Running his fingers through his hair, he says, "Wanna go in? I'll buy ya a book?" Tossing her hair back, she says, "Nah, I already have one."

—⁓—

Be bold. Make no easy mistakes.

—⁓—

Of the beauty of the well-said—

—⁓—

To the young Ingres, Degas advised, in 1855, "Draw lines, young man, many lines!" In his diary Paul Klee reveried, "Drawing is no more than taking a line out for a walk." Matisse mused, "One must always search for the desire of the line ... Remember a line cannot exist alone, it always brings a companion along." Line after line we draw, line after line we write. Lines stretching into infinity. Unless you're stuck in a funky bar at closing, never say, *It's just a line*. Unless it is.

———

A manuscript is nothing, then something, then everything, maybe a book, maybe a life. Maybe. Maybe not.

———

Never say, "Just my imagination." Unless you can sing like The Temptations.

———

The way that is the way is no way, and that's the way it is.

———

I have been training all my life to be ready, but for what? For this, for now; for now, for this.

———

Inspiration wishes, genius does, audiences wonder.

Breviloquence, n. The secret sauce of aphorists, the merging of brevity and eloquence; the opposite of magniloquence, which is the ill-conceived desire to appear brilliant while sounding bombastic.

—⟋⟍⟋—

White-line fever. Long-distance driving's severest danger. Road hypnosis, usually at night, as opposed to the black line fever of long distance writing. Driving ourselves crazy with our own writing. Hypnotized by the blank white road of endless pages lined with the words we're laying down like drops of hot asphalt. Careful that you don't cross the line and collide with the oncoming reader—

—⟋⟍⟋—

The only thing that makes not being with you bearable is knowing that I can write to you about things I wouldn't otherwise dare to say.

—⟋⟍⟋—

The power of aphoristic writing attracts the unsaid thing like a magnet attracts iron filings, and draws out our desire to become attached to words we love by learning them by heart.

—⟋⟍⟋—

We shouldn't trust the wind at our back if we don't know where we're going.

Crisply saying what you mean. Packing all the wisdom you can muster, like Cicero's story of Alexander's miniature *Iliad*. Fifteen thousand, six hundred and ninety three lines packed into a walnut shell he could carry into battle for inspiration. That's an aphorism, in a nutshell.

—⁓—

Opining on aphorisms, Canadian poet and editor George Murray writes, "I describe them as poems without all the poetry getting in the way. But, for all I know, philosophers might describe them as thoughts without all the philosophy getting in the way." If you could distill poetry, if you could crystalize prose, it is what you would be left. First thought, best thought, but burnished by time and consideration.

—⁓—

Found poem. Flipping through yellowed pages of Youth, a selection of stories by Joseph Conrad, given to me as a gift by an old girlfriend. On a yellow slip she wrote: "To Philip, a youth often at the end of his tether, searching for the heart of darkness."Don't remember the note, don't recall her ever noticing. What else did I miss? That she never signed her name? My life told in scraps of paper in old books.

A YOUNG PILGRIM CONSULTING THE ORACLE
TEMPLE OF APOLLO, DELPHI, 2008
PHOTOGRAPHY BY PHIL COUSINEAU

13

Don't ask me what I do; watch what I don't.

—ɷ—

Late 2001 journal entry for an upcoming tour to Greece.
Read a curious passage in Pausanius' *Travels Through
Greece*. Writing about the Temple of Apollo at Delphi,
the world's first writer described the custom of painting
the maxims of the Seven Sages on the walls: "Know
Thyself," "Nothing in Excess," "Long for Wisdom."
Fascinating. His interpretation was unnerving in the way
it vindicates my own obsession with memorable sayings,
even though he wrote it almost two thousand years ago:
"These were meant to be *useful* for the life of men."
Years later the word *useful* still blazes in my mind. For
years, students have asked me to repeat it in class. For
an alarming number of them, it's never occurred to them
that wisdom might be useful.

—ɷ—

The question is not whether you should disturb the
universe, but how much. After you decide that, it's no
longer a disturbing question.

—ɷ—

"Astound me." Two words, you can bet, are running
through the mind of your readers.

—ɷ—

Creativity is a question of transmuting your private
inspiration into public communication.

No words are real until you have experienced them; no experience is real until you've put it into words.

—ᴍᴍ—

In the last letter my father ever wrote to me, scrawled with a red marker in pitifully large letters, he asked, "Did my love of words inspire you?" My first thought flared with anger, *Are you nuts?* I can feel the talons of his question to this day, the way the red-veined words grabbed me by the throat, seized my breath. My first thought was *What the hell's wrong with me?* I was sure I had told him ten ways from Sunday how much his word-mania influenced me—but then again, maybe not, maybe I held back. Our relationship was a blinking contest to the bitter end. The day after he died in his sleep, clutching the first draft of my manuscript about famous last words, by chance I came across Emerson's paralyzing lines: "A man does not grow up until his father dies." An aphorism I can't track down in his collected works, though I swear I've seen it cited many times. I swear. *Did I dream it?*

—ᴍᴍ—

Richardson on Emerson by way of Van Gogh. His sentences stand out like crows in a corn field. An image burned like charcoal onto my retina.

—ᴍᴍ—

Far be it from be from me to question the writing habits of the protean and prolific Joyce Carol Oates, she of the hundred-plus books, who has tweeted nearly 30,000 times since 2012, culminating in this twisted gem: "An aphorism is a tweet with Ivy League pretensions."

—the green sleeves of summer evenings

—she spoke softly, her words swooping like a swarm of starlings

—the truest word you can say begins with a lump in your throat

I love the feeling of carrying my manuscripts in my road-burnished leather satchel even more than the feeling of holding the first copy hot off the press.

Will anyone read me in a hundred years, ten years, one? Who knows? I'm not waiting around to find out. I'm writing for my son and his children and their grandfather.

Story, n.   The world's most compact meaning-making machine.

—ↄw—

To see the invisible is the great challenge for a poet, a scientist, mystic, or philosopher, and that has not changed since the first experience of the unseen sent a shiver up someone's spine. Think of our Australopithecine ancestor in the cave scene in *2001: A Space Odyssey*, rheumy eyes dilating with awe and wonder as the sun rose, and all the other apes slept.

—ↄw—

To turn the haunted kaleidoscope and wonder who is doing the turning—

—ↄw—

To teach students to think for themselves may be the highest art of all—

—ↄw—

To think you can do it or you think you can't—you're not wrong.

—ↄw—

New words sometimes crash like surf onto the rocks of my mind. *Beautility* came to me this morning, seconds after the chime of Sunday church bells, a long way from home. *Useful* beauty? Dreamwords. Spindrift from the soul.

One generation talks to the next in parables; to the previous ones, in myths, legends, and literature; to themselves, in the headlines of the day, to the gods in dreams.

—⟊—

Hustle but don't hurry, take your time but don't wait. Otherwise, you'll get to where to never wanted to be in no time at all.

—⟊—

From the notebooks. Serendipitously, moments after writing the lines above, I find in a yellowed journal from the early '90s a chance line about drinking wine with poet Jack Gilbert after an event at Fort Mason, in San Francisco. He was talking to a group of us about life on Santorini in the '50s. His voice caught, throttled by memory. Out came a wistful phrase from a poem he'd read earlier, something about "a magnitude of beauty that allows me no peace." And me, blue-knuckled, gripping the edge of the café table, feeling faint.

—⟊—

Transport. The secret. Of art. The mystery of mysteries. How we lose ourselves to find ourselves on the page. In the canvas. Around the melody. Within the stone. During the dance. The beauty of it is the beauty of it.

Imagination. It was my wanton desire to live in uncharted realms with its sleeping beauties that condemned me to the life of writing.

— ᴕᴕ —

The write time's the right time to be with the words you love.

— ᴕᴕ —

If you're waiting for just the right time to write, you'll wait forever, where nothing ever gets done.

— ᴕᴕ —

Time, n.   The insomnia of infinity.

— ᴕᴕ —

Whatever stops time is sacred.

— ᴕᴕ —

"They lived in *the one time*," the barman at McDaid's grumbled when I asked him what was so special about the days when the likes of Behan and Kavanagh and Joyce drank from the Book of Guinnesses in his pub. "The *one time*, lad, the one time," he repeated incantatorily. His voice rising like the foam on the pint he was pouring for me.

Time is a river, eternity an ocean, and us floating on a
raft made of creaking balsa.

—ɷ—

Books are the ashes of the life that burns at white heat.

—ɷ—

Philosophy teaches us how to live, or isn't worth its
weight in ink. Case in point: the Song Dynasty collection
called *Blue Cliff Record*, which claims the ultimate
path isn't as hard as it looks: "Just avoid picking
and choosing."

—ɷ—

Beauty, n. That which radiates and provokes.

—ɷ—

Something ineffable within us believes we are immortal.
Name it or lose it.

—ɷ—

Overheard through cellophane-thin motel walls, Boise,
1976: Bogart's raspy voice from a staticky television:
"When you work for an artist you come to expect
anything." Had to write it down on the palm of my
hand, no paper being nearby. Learned it by heart before
showering the next morning. Am I living the myth, or is
the myth living me?

Joseph Joubert's indubitable genius: To see invisible
things and name them. Concisely. Novelists hated him,
essayists envied him. To teach, he wrote, is to learn twice,
so I teach him to learn thrice.

—ɷ—

All I have ever tried to do with my writing and my
teaching is to return enthusiasm to its rightful place in
the enervated world, for every day it is drained away out
of fear of the irrational life, which feels as if the plug has
been pulled on the warm bath of our passionate life.

—ɷ—

I'd quote the devil himself if he said anything I couldn't
say better myself, but it would probably start a sulfurous
war in my soul.

—ɷ—

Beauty, the pedants say, cannot be defined, the experts
claim it can barely be described. Not one to be
intimidated, Issac Asimov, or was it the mathematician,
W. A. H. Ruston, coined the word *millihelen*, after Helen
of Sparta and later Troy. *Millihelen*, a fanciful unit of
measure for otherwise unimaginable beauty. With
tongue lodged in mythic cheek, it was said to correspond
to the amount of beauty needed to launch one ship.
Imagine how spellbinding the face that launched a
thousand.

Stories know more than we do. Stories know more than stories know.

—⚬—

Everything's been said before, but since everybody falls asleep every so often, everybody needs reminding that everything important needs to be said all over again.

—⚬—

Aphorism, n. A metronome of wisdom. A pithy saying in rhythm, swinging back and forth from the personal to the universal, helping us keep time with the timeless.

—⚬—

Our words are roads that lead to deeds, or not, choices at the crossroads. If you say you had to take this road or that road, you will be right and you will be wrong, and it won't matter because it will be your choice and no other.

—⚬—

Imagine, if you will. Crystals glowing in a dark cave. That is the image the Nobel Prize-nominated biochemist asked me to visualize if I was to have any idea where his ideas came from. As crystals suddenly brightening up a fathoms-deep cave that he was exploring without a headlamp.

Emerson. *I grind my sentences.* Was it the lover of lenses in him, or his passion for the local mill where he learned to grind the grain of his words? The verb emboldens, as all verbs should.

—⚭—

Your story is a riddle turned inside out that asks a question as it unfolds the mystery of your life, which you may never understand but you are permitted to gaze at in awe.

—⚭—

The function of the mind is to identify; of the imagination, to strangify.

—⚭—

I have always lived with a stranger in my soul. I can't get him to leave. So I've been building a room for him in the attic. It's taking forever.

—⚭—

The secret dream, the strange advice. Get lost in your work. My father's advice, my coach's advice, my first newspaper editor's advice: Get lost. Hell, no, I would scream back, I know what I'm doing. Now I tell my students: *Strangify, if you want to edify.*

THE TUNNEL AT THE END OF THE LIGHT
TEMPLE OF APOLLO, DIDYMA, TURKEY, 2014
PHOTOGRAPHY: PHIL COUSINEAU

The secret of life is not so secret. But I've been sworn to secrecy and cannot divulge what it is.

—ᴍ—

To name things is the first thing for a writer, what granting color to things is what a painter must do. No name, no soul; no color, no spirit. No thing, nothing.

—ᴍ—

If it's not impossible, it could be on the way to possible, which is the *compossible*. Possibly.

—ᴍ—

Going to the movies alone is one of life's guilty pleasures, guilty because someone we love may be hurt because we didn't ask them to go with us, or guilty because we needed the dark balm of being alone in a crowd of strangers.

—ᴍ—

Robert, the one-legged, stout-hearted psychologist confided to me that Jung himself divulged to him the secret of alchemy: *Do something every day that touches the infinite*, Jung told him while tamping his pipe. Like all secrets, it was a bittersweet revelation.

—ᴍ—

If it doesn't matter, it doesn't count; if it counts, it might matter.

—〰—

It's not possible to have a perfect day unless you have done something for somebody else who may or may not ever know who helped them.

—〰—

You know you're in trouble if you find yourself walking around in circles and someone tells you that what you're looking for is just around the corner.

—〰—

The Old Man of the Woods that I encountered while canoeing the Rifle River, in Michigan, scratched the stubble on his chin and said that his wisdom didn't come from his beard. Never did say where it came from. Just said it wouldn't oughta been very wise of him to say. Two days later, a logger, sizzled on Stroh's, told me man-to-man at The Wolverine Bar, chuffed, "Hey, man, y'know what they say out here? The wind howling in your face is said to make you a wise-ass."

—〰—

Aphorisms are word-wise, or they're otherwise.

Often, my students ask me for my favorite definition of an aphorism. I can't help rolling my eyes, knowing how *oculogyric* it is of me, but I can't help it. I feel I need to be circumlocutive, roundabout. Show it, don't tell it. So I turn not to the linguists or sophists but to poets or lovers, or both such as Rostand's Cyrano de Bergerac. "My wit is more polished than your mustache," he said, twirling his mustache with aplomb. "The truth which I speak strikes more sparks from men's hearts than your spurs do from the cobblestones." Wit, heart, sparks, cobbles. Write, I urge students and myself, until your words glow like fireflies in a dark forest. Then it's their turn go all oculogyric on me.

—◊—

Not for nothing was the goddess of memory imagined as the mother of the muses. Nothing but the source of inspiration and that's something else.

—◊—

T. S. Eliot may have heard the mermaid singing, but I have heard the books choiring. On bookshelves since I was a pimply-faced kid lingering till dusk in the hometown library. When I confessed as much to the head librarian she had the temerity to take away my library card. I was only twelve but I knew jealousy when I saw it.

—◊—

"The flabby wine-skin of his brain
Yield to some pathologic strain, And voids from its
unstored abysm The driblet of an aphorism."
        —Ambrose Bierce, "The Mad Philosopher"

—⁕—

I am thirsty for a drink from the fountain of memory.

—⁕—

The Theater of Memory offers a stage to recall the story
of your life.

—⁕—

You can't teach depth; you can only unteach it.

—⁕—

If something doesn't matter, it anti-matters.

—⁕—

If it doesn't matter, it doesn't count; if it counts, it
might matter.

—⁕—

From *The Art of Worldly Wisdom*, in 1647, Baltasar
Gracián. "Good things when short are twice as good."
A Spanish aphorism with the click of the flamenco
dancer's heel on a hardwood floor.

The real life is worth striving for, really; the spurious should spur us on.

—◊◊◊—

The murmur of a mellifluous phrase melodizes a discordant conversation.

—◊◊◊—

From the travel journals. Belgrade, Serbia, 1993. Walking around Belgrade, I remember back to the war, hearing how the librarian ran through the bullet-strafed streets to see what he could salvage, walked through the fallen front door as the great dome fell around him, and lifted his hand to catch a single page of singed paper, which crumbled, vaporized in his hand. There and then, he decided to rebuild after the war.

—◊◊◊—

The well-lived life has nothing to do with getting what you want, it's got to do with wanting what you get. Get it, got it? Good.

—◊◊◊—

My God, let it never be said of me what Sam Goldwyn said of Henry Cohen, "He never learned to live." Where does that roiling fear come from, the tremor of doubt about the unlived life? *Soulrust*. We rust from within when we live passionless lives.

Found poem. A ripped corner of a diner napkin. Faint letters at the top spell out "The Dearborn Inn." Reading it now feels like a stiletto in the heart, taking me back thirty years, to the late fifties. In flickering Bic pen dark ink I seem to have scrawled something during one of my late-night bar reveries: *What did the boy see? The boy saw his father lean over his new Brownie camera like Father Haney bowing to the tabernacle at Sunday mass, hearing his father say to his wife, who has just heard that her father died, "Don't move, darling. You're beautiful as you are. Don't move—"* She never moved for him again.

—◊—

You are not entitled to happiness, nor are you required to achieve it.

—◊—

What I love best about the best aphorisms is they aren't ungainsayable; you can gain a lot by saying they contradict themselves, which doesn't make them any less true.

—◊—

Optimism optimizes the chances that happiness will happen. Our life is characterized there, in the mysterious overlap, of chance and choice.

—◊—

There is a little starlight in all of us; the rest is moonshine. So shine on, you crazy diamond.

—〰—

"Collective effervescence." A sparkling anthropological term for what is witnessed at pilgrimage sites, the Kumbh Mela, Santiago de Compostela, Rumi's tomb in Konya, Emily Dickinson's home, Gettysburg, the Cooperstown Baseball Hall of Fame. The ecstasy of arrival, says the weary pilgrim. The gasp from a room of effervescing readers, says the wistful writer.

—〰—

There are three secrets to leading a life of happiness. Unfortunately, nobody can say what they are, though they have an inkling, sometimes a notion, always a suspicion.

—〰—

"This will be the week that was," my mother used to say when she dressed us for school every Monday morning, and then "That was the week that wasn't," she would say while putting our lunch boxes away every Friday afternoon.

—〰—

Since I try to catch whatever the wind is throwing my way—

I think best when night reaches low noon.

———

Once it was believed that "I think, therefore I am." Now it's believed that "I am connected, therefore I am." Believe it or not, neither is believable.

———

To make up for being transitory, happiness is intensitory.

———

The highest achievement of a teacher is to become an *animateur*. Someone who *animates* the material. Evokes the soul of the thing, makes it come alive. Pygmalion without the penchant for falling in love with your own genius.

———

Humor, n. Facility with *smirkwords*. A lever for lifting words into the empyrean of laughter and joy. Together, you get the centaur of aphorisms, the *humophor*, the humorous aphorism. I am told new words are usually coined by anonymous authors; we shall see.

———

Until you change your tires, the nurse warned me, you'll always be tired.

A honeycomb is none of your bee's wax.

She called him on the odd night just to get even.

You can't walk on one leg, but you can go out on a limb.

My bookshelves groan under the weight of my journals, diaries, travel logs, beer coasters, and café napkins with barely decipherable words. "Total heavyosity," as Woody Allen moaned in "Annie Hall." Recently I found a photo I took of the palm of my left hand after drinking with Van Morrison till dawn at O'Reilly's pub in North Beach. Only barely decipherable splotches of ink remained. "A little of him was too fucking much," yer Man complained about the horn player he let go after a gig at the Masonic Auditorium that night.

Later, she said you've got to stop calling me, so I stared at her from a thousand miles away just to annoy her.

And so the story runs—
and so we chase it down
to grab it by the tale.

When I understand my life, it feels like it's happening to someone else; when I don't understand my life, it seems like it could only be happening to me and nobody else.

———ɷ———

Philosophy is the art of finding a black cat in a dark room; psychology the art of capturing a black python in a dark sewer; mythology the art of drawing a dragon in a dark dungeon.

———ɷ———

Another night of splintered dreams. Shadows in the attic, shadows in the basement. Hints of hiddenness. Fear of platitudes. Flat, vapid, worn-out aphorisms, hackneyed maxims, fake interviews, cults of celebrity. Why say anything if no one is listening, or watching, or touching? I rub my eyes, open the curtains, see the tower on the hill, open a tattered leather journal and write, "Quit whining. What was I born to do? Not that, not that, this, this. This is what I was born to do. If one person reads me, reads this, I am doing what I was born to—reach others who are also groping in the dark.

———ɷ———

You descend willingly into the underworld, or the gods will open the trap door for you.

———ɷ———

Either God has no sense of humor or a wicked one.

MIDNIGHT SHADOW-FRETTED MONASTERY
HOTEL ST. YVES, CHARTRES, FRANCE, 2016
PHOTOGRAPHY BY PHIL COUSINEAU

I'm at a crossroads because I tripped over the fork in the road. I just should have taken it.

—◊—

Scavenging for metaphors, beachcombing for parables.

—◊—

Hence the grasping in these shadow-fretted pages that often resembles what the luminous poet Milosz described as the "groping for an unseen, transcendent reality." Not an evasion of this one, but an experience of the other one *beside* this one.

—◊—

The stillness of the world before clocks. When the first public clock was installed atop the shadow-strewn castle tower in Prague, pilgrims came from all over Europe to see time move before their very eyes. The ominous ratcheting forward felt like the end of time, and the gasps were heard round the world.

—◊—

"Hell without the fire extinguishers," the vet on the park bench sneered, remembering the Battle of Khe Sanh. I gave him a buck for the sudden poem. They're everywhere if you lean in and listen.

—◊—

Cobblestones, n. Larger than a pebble, smaller than a boulder, rough-hewn, worn down by time, burnished by footfalls. Beautiful to behold, but slippery when wet; bumpy, but reliable enough to help us homeward. We can stub our toes on a poorly laid stone, just as we can fall and lose our balance over an ill-chosen word. If we do, it pays to stop and look at what tripped us, as advised in the Arabian Night's tales, "Where you stumble, there is your gold." By a certain ricochet in the mind, we can think of maxims as well-trod paths, and adages like paved roads, while aphorisms resemble cobblestoned roads. Well-rounded, beautifully burnished cobbles provide some of our oldest pathways, as aphorisms are counted among our oldest recorded thoughts. Wisdom of a bumpy sort.

—⁂—

Wishing don't make it so, nor does knowing what ain't so.

—⁂—

Racked with loneliness on a long drive across Saskatchewan, late 2014. At an old neon-ribboned diner, outside Moose Jaw, I read on the back of the menu how pioneers round these parts placed lanterns in the windows of abandoned cabins to make them feel less lonely. Irony of ironies. What kind of lantern, I'm dying to ask the flirty waitress but she's staring out the window, chewing on a fingernail, then staring at her watch, waiting for someone who she knows is never coming.

Once upon a time someone pulled me aside at a party and whispered that he knew something no one else in the history of the universe has ever known. Taxi! I yelled, and fled. So should you if someone claims as much.

———

As a matter of fact, fate is a matter of chance, while destiny is a matter of choice. Your lot in life is a whole lotta luck. The rest is a grind. You can count on it.

———

I keep changing my mind because the other one keeps wearing out.

———

To save myself after four years of incarceration in a Detroit steel factory, I had one thing to hold onto: my story. Didn't feel like much at the time, but in time it did—when others saw their own story of imprisonment in mine. How prophetic it was for the anonymous poet who penned Detroit's motto, written in Latin, in 1820: "*Speramus meliora; resurget cineribus.*" We hope for better things, to rise from the ashes." Still, we hope.

———

What I am aiming towards in my writing has something to do with achieving a stillness in the midst of chaos, a kind of holy attention to divine detail.

Chasing the hounds out of my soul with the whip of
terrifying stories—

—⚬—

Once, on late night radio, an interviewer had the
temerity to ask me why I bothered to write when people
didn't bother to read anymore. Challenged, I surprised
myself by saying that writing is just what happened
when I wanted to convey what it meant to be alive. To
my everlasting shame, I neglected to say that sometimes
I needed to convey what it meant not to feel alive, as
good as dead, bruised by the punches that life threw my
way. "Oh, cool," my interlocutor, replied. Then, dead air.

—⚬—

Hearing someone tell me I can't do something tightens
my resolve to prove them wrong.

—⚬—

Once upon a time in America. Emerson enmeshed at his
Concord home with a fraternity of writers locked in a
fever dream literary debate. When a wagonload of
firewood arrived the sagacious philosopher listened
intently to the wheels squeaking outside his window
and the neighing of the dray horses. Unfazed by the
interruption, he gazed out the window and murmured to
no one in particular, "We must deal with this just as if it
is real." As all sages know, everything real is something
else, besides.

You were granted your lot in life by chance by the gods, so lotsa luck.

—⟨⟨⟨—

Until our era of shrink-wrapped attention spans there were no complaints about the length of ballads, sonnets, song lyrics or haiku, or sweet somethings between lovers. So why all the wisecracks about aphorisms as a symptom of short attention spans?

—⟨⟨⟨—

Cold fingers running up and down my spine. Scootch over. Let me tell you why it hurts so good.

—⟨⟨⟨—

Writing a book is like making whiskey from a hot steaming still hidden in the hills. Dangerous but intoxicating. You could be busted at any minute but if some varmint wants to leave a dollar on the tree stump outside my cabin I will be thrilled to leave something dangerously delicious there for them to pick up tomorrow. If it ain't a little risky, what's the point?

—⟨⟨⟨—

Writing a story sets off fireworks in the writer's mind; publishing one sets off fireworks in the mind of the reader.

Fine sayings: Iridescent pearls grown in desperation due to an irritation in the oyster shells of conversation.

—⁓—

Out of the German scientist Georg Christoph Lichtenberg's Sudelbücher, or Scrapbook, of aphoristic observations, I retrieve this crumpled thought: "The epigram and the 'sentence' or proverb are plainly related to the aphorism ... a deliberately cultivated literary form, as distinct from something said briefly." Hell, wasn't there a shorter way to say that?

—⁓—

Poetry doesn't make anything happen; it makes nothing happen so something worthwhile can.

—⁓—

It's crazy, but every time I see Vermeer's "Woman in Blue Reading a Letter," I squint in hopes of reading the letter in her hand to learn what transported her from her world to his. Still, I wonder. Does the large map on the wall behind her give us a clue? I like to imagine her lover as an explorer in the Dutch Spice Islands. Who knows? The miracle of painting is the way my eyes disappear inside the canvas. The art is what appears in the space between your eyelids and the paint strokes.

—⁓—

If you think you can have it all, you're going to have a storage problem.

—␣␣—

A jolt of Joseph Joubert lightning quick wit raced through me when I read isolation is the power of the maxim. A single star gleaming in a constellation. A smile on a familiar face in a port a long way from home.

—␣␣—

A poet flirts with words, a lover seduces language.

—␣␣—

From the dream journals, November 2016. Last night I finally dug into Jung's *Red Book,* went to sleep thinking about numinous images—dreamt about wandering down Rue St Michel in Paris—in a panic—but pass a bookstore that glows like summer sunshine—I step over gold-tinged mosaics in the entrance and peer through a broken window into a room glowing with books—I wander around enchanted across rug covering new wooden floor—one of the workers stops me, takes me back and points to the floor, says he found a ceramic plate under there that had some perfectly preserved ham-and-eggs that James Joyce left behind when he was writing one of the scenes from *Ulysses* here in the bookstore. Want to see it?

You need to read a great deal before you know you can never read enough.

———

The prophets said God loves the back. They didn't say the back of what.

———

Over and over again—sixty times this week—I listen to the blues singer's sultry voice crying out about her *Love Comin' Down*, till it comes to me that's how my books are written, only when my love's comin' down, my passion for the writing life. Guess you can't build up what you don't break down. For the first time I'm thinking maybe the most entrancing music is like the most haunting painting, but instead of staring back at us it *listens* to us listening to it.

———

The most probing question I've ever heard one artist ask another was Pete Seeger challenging Bruce Springsteen, who had no idea why he was writing songs anymore. Seeger asked him to ask of his own songs, "What are you *for*?" Challenged, I now ask this of my writing students, and more, of myself, my own work. What are you *for*? If I can't hear an answer coming back at me from the void, I don't publish it.

I am most myself with my pen hovering over a piece of paper, most *not* myself when I cannot summon the courage to write one more word, one more story.

—⁓—

Writing, n. No less than leaving a mark on the cave wall, no more than the cave wall leaving a mark on us.

—⁓—

"It ain't real till it's ink," my first editor scolded me when I arrived my first night on the paper with my story still in my notes. Easy for him to say since he was an inkslinger and all my early stories were written with disappearing ink.

—⁓—

Ah, writing is easy. Anyone can do it. You see children playing with dynamite all the time.

—⁓—

You can't judge a book by its cover; you can by reading it. So open the damned thing once in a while.

—⁓—

My writer friend Mikkel's aging mother turned to him in the Emergency Room and asked, "Is this the end of the book, son?"

Writing is easy; all you do is pick the scab crusted over your soul.

—٨٨—

Language is the magic cape, your writing room the phone booth where you change identity.

—٨٨—

If I am given six months to write a book, I will spend two months sharpening my pencils, two more cleaning my erasers, then two more rewriting in my mind what I haven't even started. Which is why the damned things always take an eternity.

—٨٨—

What I aiming towards in my writing has something to do with achieving a stillness in the midst of chaos, a kind of holy attention to divine detail.

—٨٨—

Overheard through the heating vents, the sheetrockers in our basement, where I have my makeshift library of five thousand or so books. *Slap, scrape, slap* goes the sheetrock knife over the mud and the tape. Then one says to the other, "Sheesh, I just feel *smarter* being around all these books."

—٨٨—

WRITING TO SAVE MY LIFE
LA COUPOLE, PARIS, FRANCE, 1997

Make your work your play, and your play your work, and if you don't love your work, it won't work, and it sure won't play.

—∿—

I quarry for the right word, looking for the uncarved block that I can hack away at until the hidden letters appear.

—∿—

Language is the magic cape, your writing room the phone booth where you change identity.

—∿—

An aspiring writer can learn more from one penetrating biography than from a thousand workshops; even mine.

—∿—

If the moment is a gorgeous goddess, as yer man said, then the hour is a powerful god, and the year a clever, randy centaur.

—∿—

Not then, not some day, but now is the time to lead your timeless life.

Of dreams, shards in the sand of other worlds—

—⟋⟍⟍—

Every memory is an image on its way to becoming a
story—

—⟋⟍⟍—

From the notebooks. Japan Town, San Francisco.
February 2009. We had a pre-interview tea with
Buddhist scholar Robert Thurman for an upcoming
"Global Spirit" show on "The Spiritual Quest." Losing
one eye as a boy gave him inner sight, he tells us. Veers
off onto gnomic thoughts about Kerouac, Buddha, and
the Dalai Lama. The best teachers, he says, are always
three valleys away. The best student never follows the
teacher. Shaking hands goodbye, he shrugs, mumbles,
"We might as well seek for each other's happiness."

—⟋⟍⟍—

If you want something done, ask a busy person. People
with time on their hands are usually sitting on them.

—⟋⟍⟍—

As a matter of fact, fate is a matter of chance, while
destiny is a matter of choice.

—⟋⟍⟍—

Something stupendous happens to those who learn how to slip from time into eternity and back again.

—⚬—

"Forgotten truths!" thundered the crusty old scholar with the Bodhisattva smile when I asked him over lunch what he'd been trying to convey to his students over the last fifty-five years. He pounded the dining room table with his fist, fingered his white billy goat whiskers and cried, "There are truths that are unchanging and universal." He took a sip of white wine, then looked heavenward and added, "For were they not, could the truth *really* be important?" I forget what my reply was, which, as my dad used to say, just shows to go you.

—⚬—

The only people who say there's no time like the present haven't spent much time in the past or enough time in the future.

—⚬—

From the notebooks. Berkeley, CA. Fall 2008. "Dear God, I'm doing the best I can," wrote the nine-year-old boy in a note later found by his mother. "The best description of the spiritual life I have ever heard," the bewhiskered scholar told me while we worked on his memoirs.

A fact that corks the imagination bottles up the soul.

———〰———

Things are rarely what they seem because things hardly seem rare, which makes them unseemly.

———〰———

We never forget the moment when love swoops in, and we try to forget the moment when it soars away.

———〰———

"What's wrong with *me?*" she asked. "Why can't I be enough for you?" Shaking my head, I muttered, "It's not you." Then added, unrealistically, "It's *me,* no, it's *reality.* It's not enough for me." Not till much later did it hit me how pretentious I must have sounded. *Nothing's* enough, I added, making it worse. *That's why I write!* Which only made things *worser and worser,* as Lewis Carroll might have said. But not as bad as when I picked up my pen and shuffled my papers, and disappeared downstairs for three days in the loving arms of my books where I keep trying my self-exiled Joycean best to forge in the smithy of my soul some semblance of reality.

———〰———

Life consists of unraveling the advice spooled out by the threads of the fates on the loom of time.

I wonder what happens when I miss the moment—does the moment miss me? I wonder, always I wonder.

—⁓—

The well-lived life begins with the sculpture of time, carving away the unnecessary to release the necessary, and ends with the polishing of its dull surfaces.

—⁓—

This morning, my own lullaby of bird land. There is a sweet-breasted robin chirping like a clarinet outside my window. She is guarding her just-hatched chicks by singing and winging in and out of the gnarled branches of the old plum tree, planted the day after the attack on Pearl Harbor. Suddenly, the sound of her wings turns from a soft flutter to a fearful flapping—in response to an alley cat scratching from the other side of the wooden fence, desperate to find a way to reach the nest. Love on the wing, death on the march. Beauty resting on the beveled edge of terror.

—⁓—

I count myself among the cursed who believe that we turn to books to explain life to us, then to life to explain books we love. God help me.

—⁓—

—sadness creases his face as he tells you of lost chances, lost opportunities, lost loves, lost time, himself the lost soul.

—underneath every wisecrack is a much older urgency, once thrown out as a dare: *Sapere aude*, Dare to know. I dare you. Dare to be wise. Double dare you. Dare to think for yourself. Oh, forget it.

—around midnight her words came at me strobo-scopically, turning and turning round and round but appearing to move backwards, like the spokes of a wagon wheel on a stage coach, like someone moving in and out of my life—

Great books are energized like a charged cloud filled with the electricity that creates a lightning storm.

There is a mysterious overlap between physics and poetry, the search for the nothing that isn't there, then the seeking of something that is. The search for nothing always turns up something. Silence. Words. Silence. Words. The rest is, no, there is no rest for me from words.

On the silvered wings of serendipity flew this note from my friend Stuart, who knew about my peculiar affection for aphorisms. Lawrence Durrell, he wrote to me, said of his own words that here and there were "Ones to be taken from time to time as needed and allowed to dissolve in the mind." Take that, you who have been suckered-in by speed-reading.

—⟋⟋⟍—

Imperturbability. The narrow path to a life through the worrying forest. Indubitably.

—⟋⟋⟍—

To write aphoristically is to build a bridge with as few stones as possible, and still be sure you can cross over without the understanding caving in.

—⟋⟋⟍—

My four years as a backpacker tramping aimlessly along the back roads of the world were as useless as legs on a snake, and damn if I haven't missed them ever since.

—⟋⟋⟍—

I've never forgotten the pockets of brilliant blue in the glacier I climbed in the Alps when I was twenty-two, nor the strange grinding sounds as it moved below my boots, and are grinding still in my ears.

On our last night on Hydra the sky turned the color
of crushed blueberries, while whipped cream clouds
scudded over the silhouetted islands in the bay. Sparta,
Mycenae, Olympia hovered in the mountains in the
distance. The sunset tasted like ambrosia.

—∿—

Why do aphorists use *italics* so often? Their way of
leaning letters is to language what the *Leaning* Tower
of Pisa is to architecture.

—∿—

Panache, the, the last word of Cyrano. Flamboyant
confidence, brio, zest, lust for life. The lover fulfilling his
most ardent desire, which was his conquest of language
that would seduce the woman of his dreams: "I want to
depart this life with honorable steel piercing my heart
and a piercing epigram on my lips."

—∿—

"Of course, flashbacks are a thing of the past," Oscar-
winning screenwriter Waldo Salt once told me. Surprised
that I knew my Sam Goldwynisms, he added, "So I
write *mine* in real time." *Flashnows!* I thought on the
drive home, cuffing my forehead, remembering too late
to tell him that *of course* I know that everything is
happening n*ow.*

—∿—

The movies began as motion studies, the theater began as studies in emotion.

—◊—

Movie, n. A wall that comes alive. A moving story meant to move the movie-goer. Flickers of truth from the kingdom of shadows. Eternity twenty-four times a second.

—◊—

The problem with writing every day is that it cuts into my movie time.

—◊—

Words and images fight for territory in the screening room of my soul.

—◊—

Watched four movies yesterday, prepping for an upcoming workshop, fell asleep on the couch, woke up with this streamer going through my film-addled mind: *A movie a day keeps reality at bay.*

—◊—

A dark room needs a red light to see if anything develops.

I took a wrong turn down a dimly-lit hall in the labyrinthine movie studio and found a door with a sign that read: "Animation Room: Do Not Open the Door: It Lets the Light In." So I didn't. I stood in the dark until a cartoon character opened it from the inside.

—ɯ—

If you asked me why, I would say that we go to movie theaters, museums and ballparks as we once went to churches, cathedrals, and abbeys. To be stretched. So we can reach for an encounter of other worlds, heightened emotions, widened insights. We yearn for meaning, need a daily dose of transcendence.

—ɯ—

The movie is only half the story, but the story is the entire movie.

—ɯ—

I'm afraid there are frighteningly few writers who write what they think they write, I think.

—ɯ—

Call me movie illiterate, but I've never been able to figure out musicals. They start singing when they can't figure out what to say, and start dancing when they can't figure out how to walk. Guess I'll never figure it out.

BATMAN COSTUME
DC COMICS HEADQUARTERS, BURBANK CA
PHOTOGRAPHY BY PHIL COUSINEAU

If you count the 5000-year-old *I Ching,* the eminently quotable Proverbs in the Hebrew Bible, the Sanskrit sutras, and Odin's pugnacious parables, aphorisms are the oldest writing tradition of them all. If you don't count them, the wit and wisdom just doesn't add up.

—∿—

Close your eyes and see how far you can see.

—∿—

"I'm practicing perspective," whispered the great caricaturist Al Hirschfeld, wildly waving his arm, drawing in the air with his index finger, fading in and out of consciousness, dying moments later, at ninety-nine, achieving the parallax view at last.

—∿—

If you don't discover your own story, you will be at the mercy of someone who will find one for you.

—∿—

— because it hurts more *not* to write.

—∿—

— and because it's painful to pretend that beauty doesn't matter.

— so write as if your hair were on fire, but stay *cool*.
Melville. How white the whale, how black the harpoon.
Cervantes. How still the windmill, how pale the sail.

———

From the Notebooks. New York. September 12, 2001.
Yesterday I watched from Kennedy Airport as the death
planes careened into the Twin Towers. I saw the silver
starburst of death. At lunch today with Rhino, my film
partner, blocks from Ground Zero, we had to keep
brushing pulverized plaster and ground bone out of our
hair and off our jackets. We ate in screeching silence.
Tonight, I made a vow to never again go a day without
writing, but often without warning I see the planes again,
feel the crushed bones on my fingertips. Tell me, what
do you write about when you have witnessed the end of
the world?

———

Whoever said a monkey can write "Hamlet," given
enough time, hasn't spent much time monkeying around
with words.

———

The words of a holy fool are no laughing matter; they
aren't serious either.

———

Turning writing into art is easy. Cut out everything that's just good enough. It never is.

—ᨁ—

^The most daring gift we can give our children is the gift of reading so they can read right through us.

—ᨁ—

Coleridge. "The worthiest portion of our knowledge lies in aphorisms ..." Old Sam makes me wonder, as all aphorists should, where the *unworthiest* portion of our knowledge lies. Let's say it's in the anti-aphorisms. Clichés and platitudes, buzz words and weasel words. It's knee-buckling to know that so many people don't believe there's any difference, and could care less. Call them apathetic agnostics, even rebarbarative retrobates.

—ᨁ—

In ancient times a thesaurus was a treasury filled with athlete's golden trophies; in modern times, a writer's treasury is stocked with golden words.

—ᨁ—

The poetry is in the silence between words, the wave between the sea and the shore, the ripple between you and me.

A poem is the result, not the goal.

—◊◊◊—

Möbius strip, n. A twisted one-sided, one-boundaried surface. If a traveler were to saunter along such a strip, he would return to where he started without crossing an edge, without knowing the place for the first time. A phrase written along the seam down the middle of the strip would meet back at the seam—but at the other side. *Trompe l'oeil*, a trick of the eye, an illusion of three-dimensionality. *Trompe le mots*, a trick of words.

—◊◊◊—

Lines, lines, lines. Word lines, sketcher's lines, actor's lines, architect's lines. Emerson found the overlap in his essay on beauty. "The line of beauty is the line of perfect economy." In *Look Homeward, Angel*, Thomas Wolfe describes the moment that Eugene, his young hero, realizes he can read: "The line of life, the beautiful developing structure of language, that he saw flowing from his comrade's pencil." The boy's ability to read was so transportive he hid it in a "cage of mystery" and never spoke about it again. How many other children never confide to anyone about their ride on the magic carpet of words? So, too, with aphorisms, maxims, axioms. Loquaciousness crosses the line; terseness stays on this side of it. How many of us admit to another living soul how thin the line is between reading and religion. Belief in invisible worlds. Time travel. A longing for gods and monsters. Redemption.

Emerson carved sentences like Michelangelo carved marble. Montaigne painted maxims like Rothko daubed paint on panels. Dickinson sang poems like Fitzgerald belted the blues. The models we long for are all around us but we have to leave the room we're stuck in to find them.

Stories heal the soul wounds inflicted by the merciless knife of stainless steel facts.

Among myriad other things, art is a vehicle for exploring the terrifying land of beauty.

You can't stroke the whiskers of the tiger without entering its cave.

The storyteller strives to describe what is actually happening, then hints at the other things that are happening as well, things you only dreamed about. During medieval times you could not sit down to a meal until someone told a story, preferably a marvel. The appetite is best sharpened on the whetstone of a story. No marvel, no meal, no way.

Storytelling was born the first time a hunter dragged the day's fresh kill to the mouth of the cave and felt a strange desire rising in his ribcage, which came out as mumbled words to his famished family, "Wait, wait, first let me tell you what happened, *then* we'll eat—"

—⁓—

Thomas Fuller, Gnomologia, 1772. I know, I know. The enigmatic word comes from the Greek gnómé, meaning "to know, maxim, or wise sayings couched in figurative language, giving rise to gnosis. Fuller's collection is a humble hodgepodge of wisdom sayings, and the oddments of his time. The chrestomath writes, "All that I take upon me here is only to throw together a vast confused heap of unsorted things, old and new, which you may pick over and make use of, according to your judgment and pleasure." Still, the wordmonger in me hopes that gnosis inspired those gnomes couched alongside our garden paths.

—⁓—

Sheesh, didn't anybody tell you that your information can snuff out your knowledge, and your knowledge can choke your wisdom—but your *story* lets you breathe again? Unless you are a bullyscribbler who gives everybody who hears or reads him the collywobbles. In that case keep it to yourself.

—⁓—

If you're creative, it's a good idea to throw away the work that isn't working along with the morning coffee grounds. Bitterness spreads.

—⟋⟍—

Why teach, they ask, and I say, to give my students a taste of the other world.

—⟋⟍—

The ancients warned that when you draw a dragon, you should dot its eyes. I wonder why, don't you?

—⟋⟍—

Jean Rostand, the anti-aphorist and social scold, wrote in his admittedly vain *De la vanite*, "There are things which don't deserve to be said briefly."

—⟋⟍—

"Make it your own," was Joe Campbell's avuncular advice to me one night while under a Glenlivet glow. San Diego, fall of '84. The prince of mythic aphorisms condensed a lifetime of mentoring down to four words that changed nothing and everything. Only because I made it my own, not his.

—⟋⟍—

Apprenticeship, n. One who works for another to learn a trade or an art. Andrea del Verrocchio, master to the young apprentice, Leonardo Da Vinci, admonished him to lift himself out of a menacing case of melancholia: "People of accomplishment rarely sit back and let things happen to them; they go out and happen to things." That's not happenstance, that's transcendence.

—◊◊◊—

The difference between a mentor and a guru is the difference between *Be yourself* and *Be like me.*

—◊◊◊—

To teach in a selfless way in the most selfless way possible, point your thumb over your shoulder to the dark forest where there is no way or path and where you left no footprints, and hope your students will find their own way.

—◊◊◊—

Over drinks one night in Venice with my friend, the art historian and bon vivant, Alexander Eliot, who reveled in ribald stories. "Dali told me that he wouldn't mind if he went blind. Twirling his mustache, and grinning maniacally, Dali growled that he would simply press hard on his eyelids with his thumbs till he saw stars, which he would then paint from memory." Clinking glasses, Alex added with a flourish, "We're as blind as we want to be."

65

Under the blue and gold UCLA logo on his letterhead, the legendary basketball coach scrawled a brief endorsement for my book on the Olympics then added, "I hope I've taught you something you can teach somebody else." I hope so, too, Coach.

—◊◊◊—

Show me who you quote and I'll tell you who you are. Don't show me who are quoting and you will show me who you're not.

—◊◊◊—

My Greek co-leader on a tour around Greece described me to the group as a Filling Station of the Mind, which was flattering until I ran out of gas and blew a gasket.

—◊◊◊—

From the travel journals. Los Angeles, 2004. As we shook hands in the Green Room, Mr. Bradbury asked me what I was working on and I mumbled something inane about a book on the Venus de Milo that had already taken me over eight years. "That's crazy," he chuckled. "You can't wait forever—you've got to jump off the cliff and build your wings on the way down." Fiercely, he gripped my hand as if to give me the surge I needed. "Hell, Kurt tries to take credit for that, but I said it *first*. Or maybe it was the Scotch talking?"

I keep coming around to the marvelous fact that
encyclopedic means far more than "smart" or
"intelligent," definitions that don't get you anywhere
or tell you anything you can't find out in a dictionary.
No, the roots of *encyclopedia* reveal the sense of
"training in a circle," as in a well-rounded education
of both art and science, which just might get you
somewhere. If you learn how to turn circles into spirals,
which takes you into the heart of the matter.

—⁓—

Learn ten things,
forget nine,
teach ten things,
coach ten more.

—⁓—

There is phrase I hope to God I say to myself whenever
I crack open a new book: *I'm learning something new
on every page.*

—⁓—

Coming around to the lacerating possibility that the
source of depression is not being who we really are.

—⁓—

A great story should have one foot in eternity and one
in the bookstore.

MENTOR EXTRAORDINAIRE
ALEXANDER ELIOT, LEGENDARY ART CRITIC
APHRODITE AND THE GODS OF LOVE EXHIBITION,
THE GETTY MUSEUM, MALIBU, CA., 2012
PHOTOGRAPHY BY PHIL COUSINEAU

My head hurts from the fists of untold stories pummeling the inside of my head, demanding to get out. If you could see my soul, you'd see it's bruised-boxer-blue.

—⚬⚬⚬—

Unfortunately, the word *apothegm* makes me think of *phlegm*, rather than what it is, a *word* gem, or as one wag would have it, a quintessential extract of wit and wisdom, or pithier yet, a short instructive saying, which is to say, a teaching with the fewest possible words, such as the Roman saying, "*Festina lente,*" or "Hasten slowly." See what I mean? Fifty-nine words, when I could have used two: "Teach briefly."

—⚬⚬⚬—

From the notebooks, Los Angeles, 1986. The famous teacher was annoyed today by the cloying Q & A from his New Age audience. They had come for a lecture about Buddhist compassion, but several people were clamoring for exceptions to the rule, making the case for revenge against one perceived enemy after the other. The teacher threw his hands up the air, and exasperated, he asked: "How far does your compassion reach? If you can see the outermost limits, you aren't seeing far enough, and it isn't compassion you are feeling. It's your own sentimentality." As one, the audience squirmed like an octopus slithering into a small crevice between stones on the ocean floor so it can hide until the predator passes by.

Quite possibly the kindest aphorism ever penned is Emerson's reflection after a long walk-and-talk with Hawthorne. "A friend is a person with whom I may be sincere."

—⁓—

The words in my life form an uncanny tapestry of obsession interlaced with threads of happiness, interwoven with torment. A strange sight to behold by day, a terrifying one by night. Not to one to hang on my wall. It would scare the children.

—⁓—

My mind is overstuffed with underwritten thoughts.

—⁓—

I don't go anywhere without my journal, which is only fair since it never goes anywhere without me. Not anywhere I know about.

—⁓—

The Great Bazaar, Istanbul, Turkey, 1997. Combing through an ancient text by the sublime first-century philosopher, Philo of Alexandria, startled by a single line that glistens with truth: "Be kind to everyone you meet for they, too, are also enduring a fierce struggle."

—⁓—

Everyone, Philo wrote, *everyone*. You don't get to choose.
Twenty centuries later, the aphorism vibrates in me like
a tuning fork. The real thing shivers in your eardrum long
after you first heard it, which, believe me, is not the same
thing as earworm songs, those cursed ditties you can
never get out of your head. Not the same thing at all.
But I like to think that Philo's line would be a great refrain,
something Leonard or Van or Sarah could sing until you
could never get it out of your soul.

—⟋⟍—

From the notebooks. Ukiah, California, fall 1977.
Afternoon tea with the eighty-seven-year-old school-
teacher Edith Hilton, childhood friend of D. H. Lawrence.
Still an upstart crow when it comes to interviewing, I
simply ask her, like a simpleton, I'm afraid, what *he* was
like, if *he* ever talked about his books. She primps her hair,
says in a posh Lancashire accent, if there is such a thing,
"*Tremulations on the ether.*" The word throws me. I ask
her to repeat the phrase, thinking I misheard her. "Sorry,
m'am?" Undaunted, she expands, "D. H.L. said the novel
was a *tremulation* that can make one more alive, make
one *tremble.*" We spoke for four more hours, over an
endless train of teacups, about the Suffragette movement,
the shunning of D.H.L. by the London literary snobs, and
the Sunday teas her parents staged for Orwell and Shaw
and Woolf. I only caught half it. My mind kept going back
to that word, that word before which I tremble still.

—⟋⟍—

71

You can't cut corners with your character; character is what time cuts into your face, the truth be known, from its roots in *kharacter,* the ancient Greek chisel that sculptors used to cut inscriptions into stone.

—⚬—

What I look for in a work of art is the selfsame spirit that flows through the single blade of grass shooting up through a crack in the sidewalk. The green force, the fierce desire, the ferocious push and pull of *lived life.*

—⚬—

And what of the sweet pleasure that comes from recognizing an old friend approaching you, her marmoreal shoulders gleaming, her red hair sending off solar flares, her head tilted in angles of thought. You know her long before she speaks what she has already said.

—⚬—

Everyone is an artist, not everybody is creative. Not really.

—⚬—

Once, my mother described her hard day of working on her watercolors as *paint-stakingly* difficult. "Or what have you be," she added, in her inimitable grammar. Gently, I laughed, not wanting to correct her luminous use of words. Criticism would have crushed her.

On the importance of earnestly keeping notebooks. After Emerson gently chided him to write everything down, his friend George Peabody relented and wrote, "He advised me to keep a manuscript book and write down every train of thought ... and when I wanted to make up an article—there were all my thoughts, ready." *Train of thought.* And then I heard the *clickety-clack* of the long train of his mind as it pulled into the many-room station of his great soul.

—⁂—

From the notebooks: Paris, France. Spring, 2010. "How does the lodestone draw iron," asks Evan Connell, Jr., "if not by love?" Beauty finds its soul through love. If you've lost your soul, Gauguin told Van Gogh, try believing in your art again. Vincent couldn't hear him for the screeching in his ears, so he cut one off. Beauty, love, and soul. The eternal red triangle.

—⁂—

Museum, n. The original curiosity shop, the home of the nine muses. Carved into the lintel of the first one, in Alexandria, were the telling words: "The Place for the Care of the Soul." Read: You will find here the traces of the quickening of the culture, in scrolls, mosaics, sculptures. Tread softly for you tread on sacred ground.

—⁂—

Taking a walk scrubs the rust off the soul.

—⟋⟍⟍⟍—

A true work of art is a thing beautifully conceived and inconceivably created.

—⟋⟍⟍⟍—

Soul is the mystery that is no mystery. There in the overlap of the inner and the outer worlds, visible in the whorls left on your fingertips, and the twirl of hair on the top of your skull. Long has it been believed these were traces left by the swirling breath of the gods that whirled into your mother's womb, leaving whorls of life. *Soul* and *breath* are synonymous words in cultures the world over. Linguistic evidence of the moment of your *quickening*.

—⟋⟍⟍⟍—

From the notebooks. Los Angeles. Spring, 2004. A shake-me-wake-me morning with a boyhood hero. Can't scarcely believe I just spent an hour in the Green Room then two hours next to Ray Bradbury on stage at the LA Book Fair. Signing our new books, talking old books. Later, back stage, he bubbled like just-poured champagne telling me ("Pshaw!") the reason he's been so prolific (111 books!!!) is that he found a way to go back to his own personal myth, back to the root system of his writing life. His eyes sparkled in the cool shadows

behind the stage curtain and its rude klieg lights. I
thought of the time I was kid and thought I'd been
blinded by the Christmas tree tinsel. "It's not just going
back to your childhood," he said, blithely. "Hell, anyone
can do that. It's not just your childhood, but all the
things that ever gave some meaning to your life that are
important." I hope I got that quote right because I was
distracted for a few seconds by his wheelchair, and the
way he winced when he shifted his weight. I had to close
my eyes several times, my odd way of burning words
onto my retinas. Suddenly, I was twelve again, in the
Wayne Library, reading "A Sound of Thunder" alone,
in the fading light, time traveling with Ray Bradbury.
No wonder I felt like I'd known him all my life.

—∿—

Art is the earning of a great yearning.

—∿—

The nascent science of quotology states that we quote
others in order to express ourselves better. Emerson is
its prophet: "Every book is a quotation, and every
house is a quotation out of all forests and mines and
stone quarries, and every man is a quotation from all his
ancestors." To quote is to learn worthwhile words by
heart, to *record* is to pull something through the heart,
not to impress or depress others, but to move the soul
from doubt to wonder. One good turn of phrase
deserves another.

Strange to say, tonight the Van Gogh stars above the Provence village of Draguignan are pinwheeling in the night sky. If I stare at them too long, I'll go nuts.

———

To ask why a writer why she writes makes as much sense as asking why she breathes. Sappho, the Tenth Muse, wrote, "Although they are only breath, the words that I command are immortal." If breath is soul, and soul is breath, as every poet knows, then words are the soul of breath, and words are what the soul *sounds* like.

———

Art, n. What we make more real than reality so we don't die of the unreal.

———

From the travel journals. St. Petersburg, Russia, 1993. A walk across this starkly beautiful city to the Kunstkamera, Czar Peter the Great's memorial to the bizarre and exotic. While meandering through it today I thought of it as if I was in a script meeting: Imagine, I would pitch the studio heads: Imagine the Winchester Mystery House merging with Oxford's Ashmolean Museum. Their love child might resemble the Russian czar's haunted house collection of pickled fetuses, unicorn horns, skeletons crying over their own deaths with handkerchiefs made of brain tissue. All these curiosities housed in sleek wooden cabinets, hence cabinets of curiosity. Ostensibly, collected and erected to widen the knowledge of the then profoundly isolated Russian people. Today, his *wunderkammer* is a hodgepodge of confusion, revulsion, perplexity alongside the curiosity. And I can't take my eyes off anything here once I encounter it. Strange to say, these cabinets of wonder might be the essence of travel itself. I'm thinking of the Dutch botanist Frederik Ruysch's notion of inviting visitors to see his infamous repository of anatomical curiosities: "*Vene, vidi et judicia nil tuis oculis,*" "Come, see for yourself, believe your own eyes." Catch as catch can, see what you can, the very stuff, the marvels that make up the most memorable traveler's tales. May the gods save us from any more stories about *perfect* experiences; give us the *strangest*.

—〰—

Love is the heat lightning of our summered souls.

—〰—

Fragments are all we have of Sappho, the greatest love poet, scraps of threadbare papyrus. They are enough for now, after the slumber of centuries. The silence in the tantalizing gaps between her words reminds me of the silence between the notes of the "Moonlight Sonata," or the darkness threading through the color in Rothko's panels. Her fragments are not absences as much as they are portals. Early aphorisms.

—〰—

Xanthe, she wrote on the fingernail-sized fragment of papyrus. "Yellower than a flaming torch," the scholars read. Sappho describing the color of her daughter Cleis's hair. Papyrus wrapped around a mummified crocodile found in a garbage dump outside Cairo. The poet's longing persists after twenty-six centuries. *Xanthe.* If I could choose one word of mine to last twenty-six hundred years, which one would it to be? No hesitation there. I choose *son.* Not unlike the sun. My son. The light of his name forever fixed to the shadow of mine, mine to his.

—∿—

Museums, galleries, clubs, bookstores, and libraries provide pulsing glimpses of beauty, which make life tolerable, and small talk intolerable.

—∿—

It never dawned on me to pray for happiness; wonders, yes; marvels, surely; love, without a doubt. The chance moments of happiness have been as Carver said in the rain-loud Paris bookstore back in '87, gravy, pure gravy.

—∿—

You were so proud of yourself, juggling four lacrosse balls for forty seconds, until the fuzz-faced kid next to you tossed eight in a loop-the-loop pattern for eighty seconds. Relax. There's always someone who can juggle more than you can.

Every museum tells a story, even by not telling a thousand others.

—⁂—

Art isn't the making of something out of what you see, but the making of something others see.

—⁂—

Flinch. That's what I do when I see writers at work in a movie. I admit it. It bugs me to see them. Feverbrowed. Terror stricken over the blank page. Crumpled pages tossed at the wastebasket. *Flinch.* Clichés bother us because they are too close for comfort. It's easier to scoff at them. It's easier knowing lawyers tend to hate movies about law, doctors and nurses about medicine, ballplayers about sports. We flinch when our complexity is reduced to simplicity, which is why the physicists came up with *simplexity.*

—⁂—

Love, n. The coming together of two enchantments.

—⁂—

Love beautifies whatever it touches.

—⁂—

79

HEAD OF THE GREEK POETESS SAPPHO

ROMAN MARBLE COPY OF LOST ORIGINAL
BY GREEK SCULPTOR CRETENSE, THIRD CENTURY BCE,
NATIONAL ARCHAEOLOGICAL MUSEUM,
ISTANBUL TURKEY
PHOTOGRAPHY BY PHIL COUSINEAU

If you haven't told someone today that you love them, you are a thief.

—⟊—

The only redeemable thing about not being with you, my love, is that I can write to you and say things I wouldn't otherwise say.

—⟊—

How clever of the setting sun tonight to look like a late Turner.

—⟊—

I swear the larks outside my window have been listening to old Vaughn Williams records.

—⟊—

The most percipient comment I've ever heard in front of a painting came from a young woman describing Henri Rousseau's work at the Met, in New York, "He paints as if he's walking through a forest, singing to himself."

—⟊—

The thrill of art is *metamorphosis*, the change from the physical to the spiritual, the effable to the ineffable, entertainment to rapture, my self to my soul.

Solace, n. The comfort that laces through a grief-riddled
soul. The soothing of anxiety, the balming of blame.
What I feel when I remind myself that at least this is my
life and no other.

—⋙—

Art is no liberal conspiracy.

—⋙—

If art is a medium, why do we need "cool hunters" to tell
us what's hot?

—⋙—

Art is evidence, the path of the soul to the work. Clues
to the artist's spirit on the canvas, in the stone, around
the page, from the stage. Proof of what cannot be said
any other way, in any other court. And we can't live
without it. I dare you to try.

—⋙—

Trying to be hip is like trying to see better by squinting.

—⋙—

Watching the trends rather than the timeless is like
marveling at the weathervane while missing the sunset.

Love, kindness, and mercy; the rest is narcissism, cruelty, and palaver.

—◊—

I want to whisper to everyone I meet that a flock of starlings is called a murmuration but I'm afraid no one will hear me.

—◊—

I can hear a crash of rhinoceros, I can see an aurora of polar bears, I can smell a bouquet of flowers, but I can't touch a collective noun that captures the type of writers I know. Wait, I just typed one.

—◊—

Those who don't give naturally don't love easily.

—◊—

A library is loud with the conversations between writers of other ages.

—◊—

Whole worlds lie hidden in my notes, worlds within words. Hidden from me. Till now.

—◊—

In *The Notebooks* of that peculiar genius Joseph Joubert, he writes that we travel through memory against time, and through forgetfulness we follow its course. Resistance. Flow. Evaporation of memory, then its mysterious reappearance through the writing of it. A private eye once told me disappearing ink can be revived on parchment with a drop of juice from a sliced onion. Then he vanished.

—⟅⟆—

Would the boy I was be proud of the man I am? Ask my father, ask my son.

—⟅⟆—

Every day I look for a lost tourist or two and ask if they need help, then tell them I've never been anywhere where I didn't get lost and was grateful for any help afforded me along the way. If they seem like real travelers I give them the wrong directions. That is, if I really want to help them.

—⟅⟆—

Life is not a rehearsal; drama is the rehearsal. If you confuse the two, you will be condemned of waiting for the play to begin.

—⟅⟆—

Von Schlegel's description makes a necessary point about our pithy friend: "An aphorism ought to be entirely isolated from the surrounding world, like a little work of art and complete in itself like a hedgehog." Small, nocturnal, prickly, and rolls itself into a ball to defend itself.

—⟋⟍—

From the travel journals, Dublin, December 1974: And then all rose to their feet and lifted their glasses for the last toast of the night at O'Connor's, given by an old Country Clare woman with a lived-in face: "May you live long enough to see your children happy and to run a comb through your grandchildren's hair."

—⟋⟍—

Why do I still dream of sprinting down the asphalt lane of the long jump pit, leaping off the board and bicycling my legs in the air—straining to fly—never wanting to float back down to earth?

—⟋⟍—

What you think you want distracts you from what you already have, which is why you feel like you missed something. Guess what? Guess again.

—⟋⟍—

A strong father doesn't want to become someone his children need to lean on, but someone who makes leaning unnecessary.

—⁓—

And then his father told him he had to figure it out for himself, which of course changed everything between them, as his father knew and he didn't until he had his own son.

—⁓—

Here tell, W. H. Auden screened potential students with a simple instruction. Write an essay describing how much you love words. Reading that, my mind swerved to Shakespeare's Philip the Bastard: "Zounds! I was never so bethump'd with words since I first call'd my brother's father dad." I love mind-swerves.

—⁓—

Genius is no more than seeing things no one else sees and finding the words and images to help others see them too. No more, no less.

—⁓—

You don't understand, my aunt told me, after the divorce your father was all *suaved* up with nowhere to go.

—⁓—

My father's stoneground pronunciation of the family
name—Cousineau—carved in my soul like a chisel cutting
letters in marble. Emphasis on the coo and the no. Years
later, a distant cousin pulled me aside after my book event
in a Cleveland bookstore, after I'd revealed that my father
had told me our name meant "the cousins down by the
water." Taking a deep breath, she said that her father told
her that Cousineau hailed from the old French verb
cousiner, which meant "to move a thread between things
and people." With a shimmy in her voice, she added,
"That's you, Cuz." Our Ariadnes often arrive with threads
we never knew we needed.

—⟋⟍⟍⟋—

Eternity isn't horizontal, it's vertical, and can't be
measured in time, only in intensity.

—⟋⟍⟍⟋—

A long-lost wordless note from my father. Hidden in a
letter he sent to me when I was flailing in my twenties.
A column by L. M. Boyd. In bold red ink he underlined
an aphoristic quote by the obscenely rich John Paul Getty:
"I'd trade my fortune for just one happy marriage."
Reading that felt like an ice pick in my heart, maybe
because I knew my dad drove an old-fashioned ice truck
for high school spending money. Only then did I know
what he had been trying to tell me since I was a boy, the
icy truth about his marriage he couldn't reveal any
other way.

Strange beauty. The most irresistible because the most inexplicable.

—〰—

Beauty balms the wounded soul.

—〰—

A parable. To reach the land of happiness you must cross the isthmus between time and eternity. I have no idea what that means. I woke up this morning muttering those words to myself in the haze of hypnogogic wonder. Then I remembered that I was talking to my infant son, dandling him on my knee, hoping against hope that his old soul would remember my words. And more that he might someday know that his dad's parabolizing wish for him was that he might find for himself that lost empire.

—〰—

From the road journals. Dublin, 1986. Overheard a pub crawler at O'Donoghue's tonight, maundering into his pint of Guinness, "Gaelic? I'm told it's a grand language by thems that knows."

—〰—

Stories are maps we use to explore our amazement.

A terrible beauty is far more troublesome than a gorgeous beast.

—⚬—

We see what we want to see, and don't see what we don't want to see. So we can't see what we're not looking for, and not looking for what we don't want to see.

—⚬—

Wonders aren't always wonderful; dangers aren't always dangerous. Two sides of the same encounter is more like it. Halfway through every adventure worth the name. Take on the wonder as you would a danger, and a danger as you would a wonder, and the gods might allow you to pass by. Or they might not. Who cares.

—⚬—

Beauty provokes us to move toward the object of our enchantment.

—⚬—

Beauty is half the Golden Mean, the other half is fool's gold.

—⚬—

The beauty is in the overlap between the thing created and the mind that contemplates it.

—⁂—

An Irish parable. The Aran fisherman stood on the edge of the known world, at the far end of Inis Mor. The ruins of Dun Aengus, the Iron Age fort, were behind him, and before him was a three hundred foot cliff, which dropped down to the wild Atlantic Ocean. With his arms akimbo, he defied the fierce winds off the sea. Teetering on the cliff's edge, he slowly leaned over, bowed and doffed his green plaid cap, once, twice, three times. Standing a safe distance away, steeling myself so as not be blown over, I thought at first he might be enacting an ancient ritual, perhaps acknowledging Manannán mac Lir, the Celtic god of the sea. When he spun around his face wasn't somber. He looked happier than any man I've ever seen. I strode towards him and gently inquired why he had just done what he'd done. His wry smile suggested he was going to treat me like the village idiot. But then his face softened, his eyes sparkled, and he said something strange in a strong Aran brogue, "No load to have it, lad, no load to have it. I can bear the life here. Ah, bejaysus, will ye look at it? Just look at what I look out over every day. Isn't it the most beautiful sight you've ever seen? I used to fish those waters, as my da' fished them, and his da' before him. No more fish, no more. No load to have it. Still, it's grand, which is why I come here every day and doff my hat to the beauty of the world."

A TERRIBLE BEAUTY

ON THE ROCKS
BALLYCONNEELLY, CONNEMARA, IRELAND, 2015
PHOTOGRAPHY BY PHIL COUSINEAU

The miracle of acting is the revelation of a wave of thought as it emerges from the soul and spreads across the human face.

—⁓—

The Irish mystic confided to me that for the Irish, to "go down pub" was like going to church to confess your sins to the bartender, or ask for absolution from the bar maid, or take communion with your friends. Hug your jar as if it were a chalice, he said, lifting his likewise. Sing your songs like they were psalms. Hearing that made me want to pray over a pint.

—⁓—

Dryden defended brevity. "If you be pungent, be brief; for it is with words as with sunbeams—the more they are condensed the deeper they burn." Briefly, he meant this: It's not for lack of time we value the brevity. It's for want of more time, better spent.

—⁓—

Once upon a time, Jack London revealed how he learned to tell a story. By traveling with hoboes, he said, who learned to tell the tale that would win them a free meal —in the split second that a housewife cracked open her front door. "Ma'am excuse me, the goldarndest thing happened to me …"

—⁓—

The road to contentment is cobbled with stones walked on by those who have learned to get what they like along the way, rather than be forced to like what they get.

—⟶⟵—

Every creative act begins hot and is completed cold, at a distance, at a remove, like a crane shot in the movies, because we can never get enough perspective.

—⟶⟵—

On stage with my mentor at CIIS, San Francisco 2004. Leaning into the evening I ask him what the difference is between pleasure and happiness. "The former is transitory," he says, waving away my gadfly question. "Think of a hot bath before going to bed on a cold night. It is delicious, is it not?" I nod and egg him on, "But who would want to live in a bathtub?" Laughing like the Buddha himself, he swerves on the question and says seriously now, "My sentiments exactly. Happiness is the greater state of being because it has a longer lifespan. The question is how we can lengthen that span, or a finer point still is how can we *maximize* happiness in our lives?" "Hmm," I hum, milking the moment. "By living for something greater than ourselves?" I ask. Howling with laughter, he says, "You've been reading my books!" End of lecture, end of mentorship.

—⟶⟵—

We are rarely interested in things that stay the same, that's why we call it news. Every bit of gossip, every bulletin reminds us that everything changes.

—◊—

Seventy thousand or years ago, someone, man, woman or child, we'll never know, scrumbled around the cool dirt floor of what's now known as the Blombos Cave, which is poised on a limestone cliff with a bird's-eye-view of the Indian Ocean. Noticing a three-inch-long piece of reddish brown polished stone, this distant curious cousin of ours lifted it up with one hand and turned it around and around. *Thinking. Imagining. Visualizing.* Nearby lay a stone point, which was picked up and used to carve several lines that look now like crosshatching, along with two parallel lines and a third vertical one. Primordial scorekeeping? Antediluvian doodling? Stone Age surrealism? Call it one of the earliest known etchings. Name it as one of the earliest known works of art. Leaving a mark marks the path of our lonely but lovely evolution.

—◊—

The task of art is to respond to the cry of the soul to grow by making some- thing out of no-thing, which I think is the place that the stuff that comes out of the blue comes from.

—◊—

Religion is about love and kindness and forgiveness—or it is about nothing at all—and I forgive you if you don't kindly agree.

—⟁—

What was not included in the Baltimore catechism we were forced to read as children: the numinous notion that God made man so man could make gods.

—⟁—

Intellectual, n. Someone whose mind watches itself, observed Camus, watching other intellectuals one day in a Paris cafe. He didn't say who watched his.

—⟁—

"Peculiar grace." Thomas Merton's haunting description of the beauty of Shaker chairs, the achievement of woodworkers who, he wrote, believed an angel might come down and sit on it. Peculiar grace could also describe his own writing style, as if he believed an angel might come down and read his books, which is why his prose sang like the Psalms, and his poems had the stillness of prayer.

—⟁—

It is a wasted day if I haven't learned one new thing—and unlearned two others.

Since legends are the chimeras of literature—part history, part fantasy, and wholly charming—take them as seriously as you would take a dream. Not literally, but symbolically—as signs from behind the scrim, the back of beyond. Or not. Just never say, *just* a symbol, although that would make a good story, too.

—⟋⟋⟍—

The poet fiddles with words, the painter trumpets with colors, the actor drums with his body.

—⟋⟋⟍—

The roots of despair reach down to the realization that we are not who we think we really are and we don't know why.

—⟋⟋⟍—

All great art moves *you* because the artist was moved. Her paint pulsates on the canvas, her chords are flung through the air, her words wend their way from her heart to yours. The art spirit moves from her to you, sometimes back again, in spirals, whirled without end, which is why you swoon.

—⟋⟋⟍—

The trouble with D. was he was so deep he was superficial, which just made him unfathomable to the rest of us.

We had nothing more to say to each other and we said it. Chivalry may not be dead, but gallantry can get you killed.

—〰—

Depression is a black moon rising, a blood-red sun setting, below the horizon of your soul.

—〰—

A found poem, a single line, a world, scavenged from an ancient pilgrim's guide, and inspired my book on sacred travel: "Pass by that which you do not love." That thousand-year-old aphorism has compelled more people to write me, from Lithuania to Uruguay, pleading with me to tell them what it means. Always by hand, I write rhapsodies on the theme of this: "If your journey is meant to be the trip of a lifetime, beware for the road is rife with distractions that will pull you off center; if you don't love it, pass it by, without judgment, without scorn. Keep moving until you find what you do love."

—〰—

Book larnin'. My driver in the hollars outside Asheville explaining why the preachers up in the mountains were suspicious about books. "It ain't the books, it's the book larnin,'" is his corrective to me. "If there ain't no Holy Ghost in the pages there, they say that there ain't no need of it."

Seriously, she said. Why do you write? Seriously, I said.
If I don't, I don't pay attention. Seriously, she asked
again. You're not paying attention, I said as she looked
at herself in the mirror, now worried I was going to
write about her.

—⟋⟍⟍⟋—

The only way to trick fate is to take it into your hands
and transform it into something more: destiny. You meet
it on the road you took to avoid it.

—⟋⟍⟍⟋—

Fate and destiny, or chance and choice? You choose.
Really, you have to.

—⟋⟍⟍⟋—

We cling to the truth of our lives like Odysseus to the
logs of his storm-tossed raft.

—⟋⟍⟍⟋—

Looking for a pencil sharpener, I ransacked my boyhood
school desk, now used by my son, and came across an
index card on which he had scrawled something that
made my eyes sting with tears. It was his definition of
speech for his fifth-grade English class. "Speech can
change reality in a variety of ways, from triggering
revolutions to influencing personal descisions [sic] and
actions." Say no more, my boy, but say no less.

Travel journal entry. Crete, 2012. This afternoon we
explored one of the Eilitheia Caves. Four levels,
hundreds of feet down into the Stygian darkness, we
hunker around a four-thousand-year-old altar to the
goddess of fertility with our Cretan guide, the passionate
Georgios Spiridakis. After ten minutes of darkness that
felt like being wrapped in black crepe paper, I asked him
what inspires him to lead groups year after year.
"*Meraki,*" he tells me, "In Greek it means passionate
creativity, what you display if your soul into your work."
My mind meanders back forty years to my parents
dancing in the living room to the bouzouki music from
Zorba the Greek—just as Georgios adds, "Like our
Kazantzakis having his Zorba say that a man needs a
little madness if he is ever going to be free." Closing my
eyes in the ancient darkness, I feel a shard of pottery
being slipped into my hand, and hear Georgios saying,
"Here is a souvenir, Minoan, I think. I give it to you
with *meraki.*"

—·∭·—

Of the ruins to come ...

—·∭·—

The ruin-seeker seeks runes, signs that evoke lost worlds.

—·∭·—

Insomnia, n. The poor man's meditation.

I hate it when one foot falls asleep and waits for the other shoe to drop.

—⚭—

I never sleep well, and I blame the friend who gave me a Buddhist alarm clock that wakes me up every five minutes.

—⚭—

During a lecture on creativity at UCLA , late '90s, I let slip that I hadn't slept much since my own college days, some thirty years before. Four or five hours a night. A student approached me during the break and handed me a piece of paper with hastily wrought numbers. If you only slept four hours a night all these years, he said breathlessly, you *earned* four extra hours every day. I multiplied forty years times three hundred sixty five days then multiplied that number times four hours. Distracted by the other hovering students, I muttered, Uh, great, so? Well, he said, that's *crazy,* dude! It means you've lived *seven* extra years longer than everyone else your age. Just making time, man, just making time.

—⚭—

An alarm clock is so dull compared to the tap on the window by a knocker-upper's bamboo stick in dear, dowdy eighteenth-century Dublin.

—⚭—

From the dream journals, late 2015. Renvyle House,
Connemara, Ireland. Strange orange moonlight wakes
me out of my slumber. Dreaming of a flower-festooned
street corner in Ennis, Ireland. Circling an ingenious
bronze machine that looks like a beautiful old,
clockwork-driven *orrery*, that's the word—where did
that come from—a glittering mechanical replica of the
solar system. Excitement vibrating through me as I
write this in the pumpkin-colored night. I'm sure I've
discovered the long-lost secret to happiness. I'm
desperate to reveal it to you, but you've disappeared.
I run down the rain-slicked cobblestone road to The Old
Ground Hotel, where you suddenly reappear in the
Poet's Corner Pub. You're the loveliest sight I've ever
seen. But you fade into an apparition—now you're
transparent—as I try to divulge the secret. I'm stricken
by the mumble-fumbles, groping in the dark for the keys,
grasping for words in the invisible dictionary. Foolish.
Oblivious. Preposterous. Can't fall back asleep. Can't
step into the same dream twice. You can only drown
in the white-water rapids of meaning rushing by.
In an idiotic world, the only way to survive is to be
radically yourself.

—∿—

Asking writers if they had a good day of writing is like
asking insomniacs if they had a good night's sleep.

—∿—

Bloviators aren't all wrong, aphorists aren't all right. It's
a twisted world.

"Those who don't know history are condemned to repeat it" is just a nice way of saying "Those who don't take the trouble to read up on the history of the world are fated to relive all the lies and stupidities of those who don't know any time other than their own."

—⟋∿⟍—

The ship of democracy founders on the dangerous rocks of a stubborn belief that your ignorance is just as important as their knowledge, your chop-logic as vital as their common sense.

—⟋∿⟍—

Political pandering is the last refuge of the scoundrel, and the first.

—⟋∿⟍—

Those who wear loud clothes make people cover their ears; wear your learning lightly. But for god's sake, wear it, or no one will hear you.

—⟋∿⟍—

Ignorance is skin-deep; foolish goes to the bone.

—⟋∿⟍—

A balled fist cannot hand over a gift.

IN THE SHADOWS OF THE SCRIPTORIUM MONASTERY OF CLONMACNOIS,
IRELAND, FOUNDED IN 544 BY SAINT CIARAN
PHOTOGRAPHY BY PHIL COUSINEAU, 2004

103

Ridicule is the last refuge of the coward, and the first.

—‒₥‒—

Crepehangers are cringeworthy.

—‒₥‒—

Stupid, adj., from PIE *stupe*-—Struck senseless,
nonsensical, as opposed to ignorant, which is simply
unknowing. A word that stretches back to the bleeding
dawn of time. Stupidity has long been the tax we pay
for ignorance, which in turn simply means not knowing.
Not knowing, senseless, and worse, not caring. A vain
agnostic illiterate.

—‒₥‒—

Political pandering is the last refuge of the scoundrel,
and the first.

—‒₥‒—

"If you had another brain, it would be lonely," he
shouted at me when I was twelve, only half-joking.
I was tempted to shout back at him that if he had
another heart it wouldn't be lonely, but I didn't dare,
telling myself I didn't want to him to have a stroke.
Then something else stopped his heart and he wasn't
lonely anymore.

The purple elephant in the room is that intelligence is riddled with doubts while idiocy bristles with confidence.

———

From the Notebooks, Caffe Trieste, San Francisco, October 2013. Overhearing Ferlinghetti being interviewed by a young exchange student from Italy. She shyly asks him what's wrong with the system in America: Growling, he says, "We're graduating illiterates now. None of them knows anything about the world ... I'm a civil Libertarian; others call me an anarchist. Ha, I thought the people who were rebelling were going to win. Now we're a computer society, which is really an anti-society. Twenty years ago you had to publish books to get ideas out there, now you just have to use the web. There's no room for integrity. Everything has to be fast, fast, fast." Growling, he asks for another glass of wine. Winking, the barista gives it to him on the house.

———

You have my resistance—but you will never have my hate.

———

A fascist thinks the bully pulpit gives him the right to ridicule anyone who doesn't appreciate the genius of his sermons.

Nothing cures loneliness better than solitude.

—⁓—

Resentment is no excuse for cruelty.

—⁓—

From the Notebooks. Athens, Greece, 2015. In ancient Greece you were a *moron*, a fool, if you didn't visit the Hill of the Muses in the morning for inspiration, and an *idios*, an idiot, if you didn't walk to the next hill, the Pynx, to do your civic duty by voting in the Senate. If you did both, you were *esokratoun*, "sokratizing," you were *becoming* a thinker. You aren't born a thinker, you become one. Think about it.

—⁓—

A stubborn clinging to the lack of information, a strange pride in unawareness, a soul-corroding strain of anti-intellectualism has been the bane of political and cultural life in the U. S. since its founding, which was marked by a disdain and a suspicion of Old World aristocratic education. Suppose that the average American was self-conscious about their lack of curiosity, and shy about their desire for self-knowledge, but I repeat myself.

—⁓—

A quiet conscience sleeps through thunder, a guilty conscience wakes up with the slightest ray of sun.

Devastating your forests, rivers, and coral reefs for a few dollars is like burning ancient scrolls to heat your house, or using mummies to stoke the engines of your locomotives, as the Egyptians did in the nineteenth century. If you're not careful, your own history goes up in smoke.

—∿∿—

Ignoble politicians flatter the uninformed for being smarter than the informed, making the world safer for bullies.

—∿∿—

Beware of the soul eaters. They'll have your wife for breakfast, your children for lunch, and you for supper.

—∿∿—

A snob is a narcissist without the benefit of a mirror.

—∿∿—

Grief, n. Dead reckoning in the soul.

—∿∿—

Dolorfuge. Grief banisher. How is it possible this dolorous word was banished from the dictionary, if not for want of use. See: nepenthe. The brew stirred by Helen, the one the Trojans called the grief-bringer, to banish the sorrow of those remembering the withering war.

Still chasing the hell-hounds out of the dark forest of
my soul—

—⟋⟍—

If somebody isn't feckless, are they *fecked*, as the Irish
are wont to say? If something can be out of whack, what
would it take to be in whack? If you can find someone
inscrutable, can you find them scrutable? We don't know
half of anything we ever talk about. But which half?

—⟋⟍—

Imagine Coltrane playing a typewriter. From *Pale Fire*
comes this heart-stopper: "stilettos of a frozen stillicide,"
his description of the death of raindrops falling off a
roof. I bother to describe this to remind myself that after
reading Nabokov there are no more excuses. If you can
see it, you can describe it, and more, give it phonetic
justice, lambent beauty. Or the language you were born
with dies on the vine of your tongue.

—⟋⟍—

Every day we need to go a little crazy just to stay sane;
that's where art comes, the crazier the better for the
insane.

—⟋⟍—

If you want to mess with a narcissist, point him toward
a hall of mirrors.

Petulantly, she asks me why I am obsessed about the past. I throw my hands up in the air like a hockey goalie trying to protect himself. *You mean you think I'm obsessed, just because I write about it?* My eyebrows do a Groucho Marx, furrowing my forehead. She pulls a face, pouting as she does when she feels misunderstood. Nothing is past if I can remember it, I say, strategically. *Fuhget about it,* she sighs, knowing we have no future.

—⟁—

Once bitten, twice shy; twice shy, forever alone.

—⟁—

If you are intimidated by the depths, the surfaces will terrify you.

—⟁—

I have never gotten over the sight of a rotting dog on the brambled edge of the woods near the house I grew up in. Gouged-out stomach, maggots, death stare. Didn't need a priest anymore to tell me what death was all about.

—⟁—

Laconics. Spartan speech. Brief, preferably monosyllabic. Concise. Effortless. Terse. The Athenians dispatched a messenger warning Sparta if it didn't surrender it would be razed to the ground. "If," came the one word reply. Say. No. More.

When you can't write, write anyway. Not because you believe you're a genius but because you believe you have a story that's worth telling. Believe it or not, that's the only reason to write, anyway.

—⟋⟍—

A travel poster is catnip to the restless.

—⟋⟍—

When you travel, every night is Friday night, every day is Saturday, and every Sunday is your eighth day of the week.

—⟋⟍—

If man is a god in ruins, ruins are where a god became a hapless man.

—⟋⟍—

When it comes to travel writing I've become lachrymose intolerant. I can't digest sentimental writing.

—⟋⟍—

Long ago, on a cliff on the west coast of Portugal, I came across petrified dinosaur tracks on the side of a cliff that rose high into the sky hung with a scimitar moon. My fingers sank into the cool dark footprints and traveled back in time for an eon or so.

The deeply rooted move more freely because they aren't always trying to get home again.

—⟋⟋⟍—

We journey to ancient sites as if trying to recall last night's dream, trying in vain to read the runes within the ruins, which in turn destroys any effort to keep up with the future.

—⟋⟋⟍—

Like Yogi says, nostalgia ain't what it used to be, though I doubt the catcher with the bulldog face knew why. Like Homer said, nostalgia was the pain the sailors and soldiers felt while trying to get home again. Now it's the pain we all feel for not being at home anywhere.

—⟋⟋⟍—

Overheard at the airport: "It took us nine hours to fly home from Jamaica to England. It took the Americans only three hours to get home. That's unfair. Them damn Yankees get all the breaks. It will be silly o'clock by the time we get home."

—⟋⟋⟍—

Go ahead, travel through unknown lands until you find your one true home, if you have one—but what if you never find it, who do you blame then?

111

The most exciting moment of any voyage is when you reach for the door handle of your home and step outside, knowing anything is possible—

—◊◊◊—

When you get to where you were going, well, there you are; when you get to where you were not expecting to go, well, even better. The effort to get from nowhere to elsewhere.

—◊◊◊—

If you don't risk getting lost, you'll never be found.

—◊◊◊—

As a kid, I believed the real life was elsewhere, cloud hidden, whereabouts unknown. Anywhere but here which felt like Nowheresville, as Maynard G. Krebs moaned over his bongos. It took girdling the globe for years to learn that no place is nowhere, elsewhere is everywhere, if you are really where you are.

—◊◊◊—

I dreamt of riding on a runaway cable car and grabbing the brake control to grind it to a squealing stop, but the metal handle turned into a pen, which exploded in my hand.

—◊◊◊—

Peace Corps volunteers call it "compassion fatigue."
Real reporters call it the "coups and earthquakes"
phenomenon. They're referring to the hugger muggered
news of the world, the jumbled mess of information.
If people don't respond or get involved, it isn't that they
don't care. We only sympathize with the tragedies of
those we can identify with. The challenge is not unlike
the invocation in a script meeting with a maniacal
producer shouting "Show don't tell!" Show folks how
what happens half a world away eventually impacts
them. Call it the butterfly effect, or the flutter-by
effect, call it what you will. But show them or they
will not care.

—⟋⟍—

We usually see what we're looking for, even when we're
not looking.

—⟋⟍—

If a time traveler meets himself at the crossroads, do
they each remember the same thing? If not, why not?
It is easier to plumb the depths of a dozen countries than
to explore the width of one true friendship.

—⟋⟍—

Today I parked in Chinatown in a space with a stenciled
fortune-cookie message: "There is still time for you to
take a different path." When I came back there was a
ticket under the wiper with a note in pencil: "Too late."

WINDY WALLS OF TROY
HISARLIK, TROY, TURKEY, 2015
PHOTOGRAPHY BY PHIL COUSINEAU

It was the crackle on old-time radio that gave us a sense of riding the airwaves, the wave of air that sound makes when it sails a great distance, that created the sense of transport.

—⟋⟍—

Friendship, n. A whetstone used to sharpen one another's character.

—⟋⟍—

From the travel journals. Cape Town, South Africa, 1999. "It was a mafficking good time," said our South African conference host, pushing back the plate of crocodile steak and impala sausages, and vigorously shaking my hand at the conclusion of the Parliament of World Religions, in Cape Town. "Brilliant, brilliant," I said, hiccupping from having eaten the ostrich egg too fast. But really I couldn't wait to get back to the hotel so I could look up *mafficking*. My host smiled raffishly, whispered in my ear so as not to embarrass me, "It's Old Dutch for celebrating boisterously." *Busted*, I thought, turning redder than the last strings of the striped zebra steak on my plate, embarrassed I'd been caught with my dictionary pants down.

—⟋⟍—

The road to the house of your friends can become overgrown from lack of attention if you take too many other roads.

115

Love travels over cobblestoned roads. Caution: slippery when wet.

—⚏—

Long, long ago, I wandered far past the pyramids of Giza, far out into the desert, without a hat, far into hallucination, where I came across a Bedouin tenderly stroking the neck of his camel, which would not budge from its comfortable spot in the sand. If I hadn't been so dizzy from the heat, I would have sworn he began singing to his camel. I lifted my hands and shoulders as to ask why, and he gazed at me wordlessly and I understood. Camels will walk, if you sing to them. Everybody knows that. He turned back, leaned down, kissed the forehead of the camel, sung his love song, and the camel unratcheted itself, legs and hump and neck and head going this way and that, a Rube Goldberg creature. As they walked away, the best of friends, the Bedouin pointed to my head, said wordlessly, Cover yourself. If you ask me to tell you anymore than this, I will not hear you. The story is enough. But if you sing to me I will tell you everything, I will follow you anywhere. Late at night, if you listen closely, the desert sand is singing. Sand grains sliding down the dunes, grinding down the night until the silence sings.

—⚏—

For those who know, no explanation is necessary; for those who don't know, no explanation is helpful.

Dreaming, v. Riding through the caverns of your mind in a glass-bottom boat with oars of gold.

—ɯ—

"The ships hung in the sky in much the same way that bricks don't," wrote the whimsical Douglas Adams in *The Hitchhiker's Guide to the Galaxy*. An image that wedged its way into my brain the night I watched the Warriors guard Stephen Curry hang in the air on the way to the rim, in much the same way that brick layers don't.

—ɯ—

Not if, but *when*. The best writing is moon-powered, words rising and falling with the tides of your will power, magically providing you with the *sensation* of the *whooshing* of seawater coming … and … going … on the beach.

—ɯ—

The hot secret of creativity is that two separate ideas collide, spark, and catch fire—and that's pretty cool.

—ɯ—

Not until you have heard the voice within things will you discover the dormant genius in everything around you.

—ɯ—

"Sherman, set the Wayback Machine," Mark and I use to joke when we were kids and we'd put the finishing touches on our refrigerator-box rocket ships. Ricocheting from one fantasy to the next, from Sky King to John Glenn, *The Angry Red Planet* to the Saturday morning cartoons, our twelve-year-old hearts soared every time the brilliant, bow-tied beagle, Dr. Peabody came on the air. We laughed till our ribs ached when he ordered his faithful pet human boy, Sherman, to set the date on their time machine to a famously awkward moment in history that they tried in vain to correct. Recently, scientists have claimed that time travelers might someday use portals to slip into parallel dimensions and visit the past. Ha, as if they've never heard of the Wayback Machine. "Hey," Mark used to warn me, "don't screw around with a kid who has his hand on the dial. I'll fix it so you were never born."

Be an original. Go back to the beginning. Bring back the fire that ignited you, the first glance from a mentor who recognized your gift. If you can pull up that moment, the incandescence of the recognition, you will never be stuck again. You were seen. Now see yourself.

Growing up on the streets of Detroit one of the hippest sayings was "What it is!" What it *was* was sudden recognition of something real in our unreal world, which made it surreal, a reason to celebrate unreasonably.

When they condensed a lifetime of living into a fistful of words—your grandmother's world jammed into an old proverb, your coach's strategy into twenty words during your twenty-second time-out, your mother doling out safety instructions to you, along with the car keys the first time she let you drive alone—they were revealing to you the face they had before you were born.

—⚬—

The purpose, the meaning of it all, you dare to ask? To get in as many shudders of joy while you can. That's how you balance the terror with the wonder.

—⚬—

There is but one way to accomplish Aristotle's own goal, a life of durable happiness, and that is living for others. No matter how unendurable that may seem. Don't worry. There are more people than you can imagine who are living for you.

—⚬—

From the notebooks. Paris, 2002. Rereading Jean Giono's classic *The Man Who Planted Trees* and underlined this as soon as I read it. "He's found a wonderful way to be happy … I am convinced that in spite of everything mankind is admirable. When you consider that all this had sprung from the hands and soul of this one man, without technical resources, you understood that men could be as effectual as God in realms other than destruction." Ever since, I've thought of notes as acorns, books as oak groves.

119

We are not so much afraid of the ending as we are of
not beginning?

———⟋⟋⟍———

There is no path to follow to your *real* work; if there is a
path it has been laid down by someone else. Your work
alone makes your path.

———⟋⟋⟍———

Life is half-over before we begin to understand the half
that is over.

———⟋⟋⟍———

Alone, adj. & adv. Life in a dangerous neighborhood.
The fear of the unlived life is an unfailing, if painful,
motivator.

———⟋⟋⟍———

It's a lost day if I haven't learned one thing—and
forgotten two others I didn't need to know in the
first place.

———⟋⟋⟍———

No one will forgive you for your good luck, just as no
one will care about your bad luck. See, it was up to you
all along, well, you and your circumstances. Lucky you.

God created the world in six days and on the seventh, wondered why.

—◊—

"As smart as can be," my Grandma Dora used to say of me, and I would flinch. Dare I say, it smarted to hear that? Even then I was thinking, *No, I can be smarter—I better be smarter—*

—◊—

The urge to write rises from the coal cellar of the soul.

—◊—

Without words, who am I? With them, who am I not?

—◊—

A poet is a lightning conductor for bolts of inspiration from who knows and who cares where; what counts are the jolts.

—◊—

The advice to my students that returns to me from them time and time again as being the subtlest but soundest shift. Not if, but when you will turn your manuscript into a book. Then not *when,* but *now.*

121

How is it that the best storytellers are the best listeners?

—◊—

If theories reflect the mind, and maxims expose the heart, aphorisms reveal the soul. That's why we are stirred to remember them.

—◊—

Who knows when time began, who doesn't know when time stopped? I say it's the moment when you told your first story because your *real* clock began right then. Conversely, the moment you stop telling your stories, your real clock stops.

—◊—

What is quotable undulates toward us in waves of calming words, and later we read and quote them to calm ourselves.

—◊—

"Less is more," the only three words I remember from Bucky Fuller's four-and-a-half-hour lecture to my philosophy class in the grand amphitheater, during my sophomore year at the University of Detroit, a campus enshrouded in barbed wire. The American Da Vinci was stalling until someone invited him to dinner and offered to take him home. Too broke for a hotel or dinner. No wonder I remembered what I did, which was less and nothing more.

Every day I ask myself how many balls I can keep in the air before they all come crashing down to earth. Every night gravity   answers: "As long as you defy me." That verb surprised me. That's why I write. To surprise the vicious censor in the schoolroom of my soul.

—∾—

The greatest antidote to self-pity is helping one person in trouble who will never know what you did for them.

—∾—

What you do for a living is your work; what you do for your soul is your vocation.

—∾—

We're lucky if we understand half the story of the words we use.

—∾—

Waiting for real life to begin turns even a sage into a fool.

—∾—

Ancient playwrights and philosophers and poets strove to reveal how wise are the holy fools; today they strive to reveal how foolish are the wise.

123

From the notebooks. Fort Mason, San Francisco. A Long Now Foundation lecture. The talk is techno-messianic, at least to my ears. I want to shout out over the auditorium: Don't let them fool you. Your mind is not a computer. If you have to believe it's mechanical, think of it as a pinball machine, for heaven's sake. Ideas ricocheting inside your skull, light up your eyeballs. Just try not to get too excited about running up the score or you will TILT! your thinking. The game that plays in your brain will shut down. Encourage your thought turns, bank your ideas, hit the flipper button when you see the next idea coming at you. Thinking should not be unfun. Twist your inborn kaleidoscope. Use the anamorphoscope you were born with to bring the fragmented truths you encounter into focus. When in doubt, bring your life into focus, or the drones will win.

—◊—

The fool who believes he is a self-made man loathes the fool who believes it's smart to wait around for Lady Luck.

—◊—

Be wary of people talking about their enlightenment; it means they can't talk about their endarkenment. That's why I love the myths. They lure us down into the underworld, and say, *Follow me—or the gods will yank you down!*

INTO THE MYSTIC
TELEGRAPH HILL, NORTH BEACH, SAN FRANCISCO, 2011
PHOTOGRAPHY BY PHIL COUSINEAU

If the Beatles were Liverpool's Ode to Joy, B. B. King was Memphis' Ode to Sorrow.

—⁓—

If you have to, fake it till you make it, as we used to taunt each other on the streets of Detroit. Trouble was, not many guys made it. Every time I make it, I think of them.

—⁓—

An actor is a magician who pulls emotions out of his hat.

—⁓—

Culture is the conversation of multitudes.

—⁓—

A true work of art is a thing beautifully done and memorably shone, usually misunderstood.

—⁓—

The piano is to music what the typewriter is to words.

—⁓—

A skirl of bagpipes in the fog, a wailing of words in the dark, belief in the melody of the unseen.

The silent pact between artist and audience. The best you can hope for is someone to nod and say, in effect, "All right, I'll look at your world for a few minutes. If I do, you better astonish me." So don't impress them, astonish them.

—⟋⟍—

Write until you know your own characters better than you know yourself.

—⟋⟍—

Work as if you're a master, demand of yourself a masterpiece.

—⟋⟍—

To be ready, to be ready, wondering if I am really ready, that is all, that is everything.

—⟋⟍—

A religious fundamentalist says you worship God in your way and I'll worship Him in *His*; a science fundamentalist insists you believe in your facts and he'll believe in *the* facts; a fundamentalist in the arts says, you love your favorite artists in your way and I'll admire the greatest ones in *their* way. Your way, my way, the way, let's call the whole thing off.

—⟋⟍—

Gauguin. His paintings he said were proof of his desire to find a lullaby of color. Sound also. "The flat sound of my wooden clogs on the cobblestones, deep, hollow, and powerful, is the note I seek in my painting." Once I read that I began to listen to paintings.

—⟋⟍⟍⟋—

From the notebooks. Heraklion, Crete, 2012. In rereading James Salter's *Solo Faces,* I find this crisp insight into my own oneiric approach to finishing a book. Salter once asked a famous solo mountain climber what he did whenever he was afraid. The climber told him he pretended he was only two feet off the ground. Rewriting my tome on the Venus de Milo for the forty-forth time over eleven years I've been pretending for a long time that about being close to the end. Now I'll think of it as holding the manuscript two feet off the floor. Maybe I'll weigh the damn thing down with my grandfather's watch so it doesn't fly away.

—⟋⟍⟍⟋—

To speak like ourselves we must never speak like our other selves—

—⟋⟍⟍⟋—

Suddenly, I've got it. Aphorisms. Sudden wisdom. Unforgettable word blasts from the great typewriter in the sky.

If you have the temerity to tell someone the job can't be done, you've lost the right to interrupt the person who had the moxie to complete it. Creativity rarely comes from sighing minds, only from crackling ones, like the way a log crackles from the release of trapped sunlight inside it.

—∭—

Last night I had a marvelous dream: I waved my hand in front of a class and left a mentor's spiral of approval in the hearts of my students. Strange, I can still feel the marks they left in mine.

—∭—

To know you, I want you to tell me what you would search for if you weren't pretending you had already found it.

—∭—

The smell of cinnamon carries me back to a breakfast I had fifty years ago, sulphur carries me forward.

—∭—

The devil might dwell in the details, but the angel is a dweller in the outline.

—∭—

I discover more about somebody in an hour of
conversation than from a lifetime of speeches.

—◊—

Myth, n. A story that tells it the way it is by telling it
in context of the way it's always been.

—◊—

If Hermes is mercurial, and Aphrodite is venereal, is
Mars marmoreal?

—◊—

In a word, *kairos* is the god of sacred time, the time
of synchronicity and opportunity, but the god also
demands of us to say the right thing at the right time,
or not at all, and so he is the god of lost time as well.

—◊—

Myth shines a spotlight in the dark corners of the
imagination; the shadow side of myth is fundamentalism.

—◊—

Labyrinth, n. The anti-maze. A tool to help those who
don't know that if they are not confused, they're not
thinking straight. It's amazing more people don't know
the difference.

Every change is labyrinthine; an encounter with what is monstrous within us, every clue a clew, a golden thread from the goddess, every escape another terror asking, *What next?*

—⟋⟍—

From the notebooks. Paris, France, 2011. Is it fair to expect art to soothe the savage beast in the human heart? Returning to Le Select after a day rummaging around the Picasso Museum. A glass of Sancerre, a slice of Roquefort and a loaf of Poilane bread. I turn back to the manuscript, my Winchester House of a manuscript, as if afraid that if I ever finish it my demons will finally kill me off. Then it hits me. Entries from my Book of Moments. Infinitesimal dots on a sheet of paper as wide as the world, points that might be connected if I can find the pattern. Picasso said that all his work left behind a pattern of dots that amounted to a Minotaur. I am looking for my monster, my god, my demon, the charcoal sketch that will reveal the outline of my life.

—⟋⟍—

I know, I know what a myth is," the little boy screams, tugging at the pant leg of the famous scholar who had just spent two hours trying to explain the meaning of myth to a crowd of breathless Jungians. "A myth a lie on the outside, and a truth on the inside."

—⟋⟍—

Myths are inoculations against the trivialization of
the imagination.

—⟴—

If you see a turtle on a fence post, do you imagine that
the god of turtles put it there? If you notice a bull's head
on a man's shoulders, do you imagine that the god of
bulls placed it there? Herodotus wrote that the
Ethiopians imagined their gods to be flat-nosed and
black, the Thracians as blue-eyed and red-haired. and
then anticipating Jonathan Swift, suggested that if horses
and cattle could draw they would depict their gods
looking like them. Remarkably, Swift wrote two
thousand years later that we have just enough religion
to make us hate each other and not enough to make
us love one another. Myth and religion provide maps
to help us to visualize the invisible, and navigate the
numinous.

—⟴—

Myth shines a spotlight in the dark corners of the
imagination; the shadow side of myth is fundamentalism.
Mythology is to religion as physics is to mathematics, a
mystery language to explain the inexplicable.

—⟴—

For the Vikings, memory was paramount. Look no
further than Odin and his two ravens. He plucked out
one of his eyes and gave it to the god Mrmir in exchange

for the gift of wisdom. Huginn represented Thought, while Muninn symbolized Memory. They flew around the world so they might report everything that might interest the god. Flights of thought, the myth says, if recalled, return home as memories. But wisdom is a gift, and for that something painful must be sacrificed. Strange to say, but I'll say it anyway. So Protean is a myth that every version of it is shape-shiftingly true, and every Procrustean insistence on stretching a myth to fit one and only one interpretation is just one more Rhadamanthine variation of fundamentalism.

The old ones said a myth is something that never happened, but always is, which is why hearing or reading or seeing one on stage or in a movie feels like you have dropped into a dream, and emerged on the other side onto a vision

—⟋⟍—

"*Wyrd* was very near," writes the anonymous monk, near the end of *Beowulf*. "Fate was at hand," we might say today, or "destiny was near." A haunting line, with the smell of the bog in it, the clang of swords, the glint of dragon's scales. An early aphorism, by any other name, because it is *always* near, but rarely named. Here, the poet did. On the single surviving vellum copy of the manuscript we can still read how the great king strode out onto the battlefield and earned the glory that made his name. We are in thrall to the poet to this day. If your heart isn't beating now, like those thunderous war drums that drove the great thane and his army, then your *wyrd* is probably not very near.

Myron's Minotaur

Roman copy of Lost Greek Group of
Theseus and Minotaur
By Myron of Eleutherae, Flourished c. 480-440 BCE,
National Archaeological Museum of Athens, 2008
Photography by Phil Cousineau

For Homer's heroes, the goal was more than victory;
the ferocious striving was to win *kleos,* glory, everlasting
fame, not only for yourself but your family, your tribe,
your city.

—⟋⟍⟍⟋—

Tragedy. A carpenter who sloughs on his last job, then
learns his foreman gives him the house he just built; a
comedy is a foreman who surprises his best carpenter
with the last house he ever built for him, not knowing
he cut corners and left a cartoon of sour milk behind
one of the plastered walls.

—⟋⟍⟍⟋—

The essence of drama is the revelation of a story
showing how to become yourself, and not someone else,
not them, which is the only story worth talking about.
Our fascination with the hero is that he is more himself
than you are yourself.

—⟋⟍⟍⟋—

The mythopoetic is the longest lasting form of art,
literally *the making of sacred* stories, but so much more,
the tying together of the inner and outer worlds, the
timeless and the timely. Conrad's *Heart of Darkness,*
Beethoven's "Eroica Symphony," Picasso's "Guernica,"
Kahlo's "Self-Portrait," Eliot's "The Four Quartets,"
Malick's "The Thin Red Line," remind us we are still
making redemptive myths.

135

A new word is a life preserver thrown to a drowning writer. *Chantepleur,* the urge to sing and cry at the same time. *Sophomania,* the unrealistic belief in one's wisdom. *Oculogyric,* the act of rolling your eyes. Catching those life lines from the dictionary helps me swim to shore. If good timing is impeccable, is bad timing *peccable?* If so, is it a mortal or a venial sin?

—⁓—

Of their own accord, Ovid wrote some two thousand years ago, putting words to the spell that comes over me in untamed moments. "*Sponte sua carmen numerous veniebat ad aptos, et quod tentabam dicere versus erat.*" "My thoughts turned into lines of their own accord, and whatever I tried to write turned into verse." There it is, the subterranean forces that make us write what it wants us to write rather than what we want to write.

—⁓—

Spindrift. One of my favorite words for the whirring sound of moist poetry, made more memorable because it was the one and only word I taught the eighty-three-year-old mythologist Joe Campbell. "Spin," he said sibilantly, then paused like droplets of ocean water before it crashes down on the rocks. "Drift," he added, his voice vanishing like smoke as we drove down Highway One. "Marvelous, marvelous to learn something new today."

—⁓—

I never did like second-hand dreams; I always wanted
first-hand memories.

—⟊⟊—

Pulviscular. Because I like the dusty, powdery sound of it.
Because I like the amplitude of words, the propulsion of
syllables, the explosion of breath when you say it.

—⟊⟊—

Ignominious, That which has no name, from ig, no;
nomon, name. The shame of remaining nameless, the
disgrace of having never been graced with one. What a
poet feels if she cannot come up with the name for what
she sees and feels.

—⟊⟊—

Sentiloquence, to conjure a word; joins feeling,
perceiving, and speaking. I needed to coin one to
describe the otherwise ineffable moment when I finally
know I'm on the right path, because I finally feel like I
can't *can't* write.

—⟊⟊—

Shivery, shuddery, quavery, quivery: the sounds of
frissons frizzling down my spine when the right word
hits home.

—⟊⟊—

The Russian-American novelist Vladimir Nabokov was
more than a writer, he was a logomancer, a man who
believed in the *magic of* words. *Rememorating* his
admiration for memorable sayings, he wrote, "There are
aphorisms that, like airplanes, stay up only while they
are in motion." The legendary lepidopterist and novelist
flung his net at the elusive butterfly of language,
capturing iridescent words, then releasing them on the
page to fly in arabesques of meaning. Nabokovian now
means: *lush, intricate, colorful;* means *words, too, can fly.*

—w—

Do not mistake me. Ideas are the wood, love the spark;
words are the ashes of a life that burns. No one but you
can find the burning point. Scrounging around the old
library of an old friend's house, the oldest in Bath,
England, feeling desolate about my own flailing writing
career, I found a fugitive line in a musty leather-bound
volume by E. Pound: "Man reading should be man
intensely alive. The book should be a ball of light in
one's hand." How did he know what I was thinking at
that beveled edge moment in time? How does anyone
know the moment you are writing lines that will move
like parabolas across time and space and land in the
unknowable future of someone else's life? There it is,
I thought that night in the whitewashed basement of
Julia's Bathwick House, better than any definition,
the power of the well-said: *Books should give off light.*

—w—

138

No matter how many or how few words you use, don't leave out the main thing you want to write about.

—⟋⟍—

Thirteen words snicker at me from the wall of the old record store in Berkeley, "It takes all day to get up— and all night to get down." Thirteen roller-coastering words to get you through the next twenty-four hours with a wall-to-wall grin.

—⟋⟍—

All day I've thought about a single line I read in *Time* magazine that the commander of the Russian submarine wrote a last letter to his wife as it silently sank to the ocean floor. In the flickering light and thinning oxygen his ink whispered, "I am writing in the dark." There must have been more to the letter, but that is all I can remember. All night I thought: *Still, he wrote, still, he wrote, still, he wrote. What the hell is your excuse?*

—⟋⟍—

Do you believe what you see, or see what you believe? It makes a difference. To see things as they are, you need to see beyond what you only see. And Edward G. Robinson snarls through his cigar smoke, "See?"

—⟋⟍—

139

The worst thing someone can say about you is that you are soulless; the best that you are soulful. No definition or theology required, just dropping a dime in the jukebox for a little Motown.

—⧜—

You were born with a spark; now you better fan the flame into a soul.

—⧜—

I'd like to give you a piece of my mind, as my Great-Grandpa Charlemagne used to say. Sometimes fragments are enough, if they lead to the larger picture. consider the marvel of the archaeologist who finds shards of baked clay tablets in the undulating desert sand and deciphers an ancient epic about a flood that predates Noah. Or the Irish farmer who spots an old leather book in the scoop of his backhoe as he digs in his sloshy peat bog, so turns off the engine and reads the muddied vellum page of an illuminated manuscript. Written, the experts tell him later, twelve-hundred-years before, and probably hidden in the bog from some invading or another. Sometimes. Fragments. Lead us into what the ancients here called "the thin places," those ghostly portals that are neither here nor there. Somewhere you never thought of looking.

—⧜—

From the notebooks: Heidelberg, Germany, 2003.
Reading Nietzsche. Seems appropriate as I try to outline
tomorrow's lecture. Amazing grace. He writes: "The
aphorism in which I am the first master among Germans,
are the forms of 'eternity.' It is my ambition to say in
ten sentences what everyone else says in a book—what
everyone else does not say in a book." Reading this, I
can't breathe, I can breathe. I must breathe. I've got an
eight-hour lecture I need to give in one.

From the notebooks. Chandler to Greenstreet to Bogart,
in *The Maltese Falcon*: "Here's to plain speaking ... I'm
a man who likes to talk to a man who likes to talk."
Brief, pithy, pointed. No wasted words for the gumshoe,
Sam Spade. We quote Hammett, quoting Bogart quoting
Spade. Herein lies the power of the aphorism: the
propulsion and exhilaration of the well-said. Plus, to
be honest, an irresistible desire to revel in their reflected
glory. Call it like it is: *suaviloquence*, the art of smooth
talking.

Last night, I came across a treasure trove tonight
rummaging through my old oak file cabinet, my notes
from the documentary I worked on in 1987 about Ishi,
the Last of the Yahi, the last of his California tribe the
gold being the transcripts of a hundred-year-old
interview in which he re-told the creation story of his
people, the last words on the last page of the interview
being: "They were taught, they were taught."

141

I am happy, *anyway,* said the sullen Sisyphus, turning to walk back down the mountain. Refusing to give his tormentor the pleasure of crushing his spirit, his smile tortured Zeus for the rest of eternity. A new world turned on that word *anyway.*

—⟋⟍—

At first, Sisyphus was relieved when he thought he heard that all he had to do was push bolder uphill.

—⟋⟍—

The gears of Sisyphus grind slowly, sometimes they ratchet backwards, leaving dark scratches on the mountainside.

—⟋⟍—

I cut myself on the jagged edge of last night's dream fragment. Down there I stumble across a lost journal in a Greek flea market. *Tantalizing,* I think, since dreams are riddled with puns. Cut to next dream fragment. An archaeological dig in the ruins of ancient Corinth. Underneath a mosaic floor I find the hidden notebooks of King Sisyphus. I pause before opening it. Will it be the outline of his book on fate and destiny? The secret behind his willful pivot at the top of the hill to return to the bottom, so he could shoulder the boulder once again? Maybe I'll find his workout schedule. Maybe his last words. I wish Camus were with me now—

It ain't an easy life, but it's my life, my boulder, I'd never dreamt of pushing any other.

—◊—

Optimism cries, *Might be, might be*; pessimism whines, *Never, never.*

—◊—

I never metamorphosis that didn't keep changing.

—◊—

Like Sisyphus, I am pushing my boulder uphill; like him, I turn, take a breath and walk back down to the bottom of the mountain, where I bend down, and without complaint put my shoulder to the boulder and push again. It could be my imagination but I'm wondering if all the ups and downs are grinding the boulder down, grain by grain, or is it just me being ground down?

—◊—

The passing strange passes by and strangifies.

—◊—

Misterioso how the music of mythology plays a different melody for every character, for without it there would be no strange transformation.

—◊—

143

The mythographers tell us that the size of the boulder
Sisyphus shouldered to the top of the mountain in the
underworld was the very same size as the one Zeus hid
behind when Sisyphus caught him seducing the daughter
of the river god. What are we to make of this? The
picture language of myth tells us we are condemned to
shoulder a burden no larger or smaller than the one the
gods think we can handle.

—∿—

Ravishing to his ear was the sound of Orpheus' lyre to
the shades in the underworld. Like Olympic athletes
training to the sound of flutes and lutes in the gymnasium,
music was solace, a gift from the gods. And so Sisyphus
kept in rhythm, kept the faith, believing that his cursed
stone was becoming bearable, by listening to the lyre of
Orpheus knowing it had the power to charm the birds
out of the trees and bring a stone to tears. Even his. So
he bore his grief and became happy, as the existentialists
believed, the music made his heart lighter. That is what I
thought of, of all things, when I heard John Lee Hooker
growl at his Boom Boom Club that the blues was three
minutes of triumph over sorrow. Hell, that's an eternity.

—∿—

Color me strange, but I woke at 3 a.m. this morning and
saw these words written in chalk on the inside of my
eyelids: Seek whatever stretches your spirit.

—∿—

A neurotic is someone who doesn't have the courage of his eccentricity.

—⟋⟍⟍⟋—

Lost in the boondocks of Northern Luzon. The old Igorot *munghuhula*, or sorceress, tells me, "You will not find him until you stop looking." I stopped. She spun a duck's egg that pointed north. I didn't ask why, just followed. I had to find myself first. By chance, we found my brother. Down in the boondocks.

—⟋⟍⟍⟋—

What is well said is well sprung, arising naturally, if there is a steady flow of energizing thoughts from the wellspring of your soul. The right words happen as happiness happens, from the well-lived life.

—⟋⟍⟍⟋—

Pochades are lightning-quick café sketches, or sudden thunderstorms of words, recorded in a moment of utter stillness. Life rendered in a one-minute story.

—⟋⟍⟍⟋—

Whenever you see a great play, you leave a part of yourself in the theater, and bring home another part.

—⟋⟍⟍⟋—

When the photograph isn't good, you need to get closer;
when a story isn't good, you need to get truer.

—⟶⟵—

Once upon a younger time, I rode my '73 Mustang up
to Muir Woods and walked around for hours all on my
own. Deep in the redwood forest I encountered the
dancer Rudolph Nureyev, also alone, sitting on a tree
stump. Draped in a floppy black hat and covered by a
black felt cape, he languorously scraped his gleaming
black boots into the red earth. Slightly, no, *imperiously*
turning, he stared at me, boring his fearless eyes into me
like a black bull gazing at a fleeting and inconsequential
bird. Nodding, I left him as he wished, undisturbed.
Later, I read that he'd said, "They pay us for our fear."

—⟶⟵—

As a young precocious young man, Ansel had to defend
his choice to pursue photography over music, telling his
dubious grandmother, "I tried to keep both arts alive,
but the camera won. I found that while the camera does
not express the soul, perhaps a photograph can." Hold
on, Ansel. As any anthropologist will tell you, a photo
can only capture your soul if it takes your breath away.
It's far from a coincidence that the words for *soul* and
breath are identical in cultures the world over. You
know the feeling, standing before "Moonrise, Hernandez,
New Mexico," or Julia Margaret Cameron's portrait of
Alfred Lord Tennyson. If it isn't breathtaking, it ain't art.

Picture this. Stalin developed a way to "disappear" people without shooting them, by hiring *retooshers*— professionals trained to retouch photographs by cutting people out of pictures in textbooks, histories, even magazines, newspapers. Now you see 'em, now you don't.

—⟋⟍—

The slow dance I always waited for at high school dances before asking the green-eyed Irish girl to trip the light fantastic with me was Aaron Neville's "Tell It Like It Is." Years later, I hung out with him back stage before a Grateful Dead concert. We smoked a joint and he told me like it was.

—⟋⟍—

If you can call a master of anxiety films "aphoristic," Alfred Hitchcock is your man, if for nothing more than communicating with short cuts and twisted endings. "Drama," he mumbled, "is real life with the dull bits left out." So should all books be, even this one.

—⟋⟍—

From John Donne to Sir Henry Wotton: "Sir, more than kisses, letters mingle souls, / For thus, friends absent speak." Notice that the man didn't write "E-mails mingle souls." Do with it what you will. Then send me a postcard.

147

SISYPHIS SHOULDERING HIS BOULDER
STREET SCULPTURE, THE PLAKA, ATHENS, 2004
PHOTOGRAPHY BY PHIL COUSINEAU

148

What we know could fill a postcard, what we don't know would stuff a post office.

———ᏗᏗᏗ———

Postcards are just the right size for aphorisms. From Pete Seeger on a card depicting the Hudson Valley, late '90s, after watching a documentary film I wrote on ecological design: "Thank you for your very fine film. It is further evidence that the happiest people I've ever known in my life were struggling ... but determined to help others, by trying to build a cooperative, a school. A new world." Which I read as him saying happiness was not won by achievement but through devotion to something bigger than them. Pete sent me another card two days later, repeating every word, but adding one, which he squeezed into the lower corner of the card. Trouble was, the card was ripped off. I'll never know what it was, but I can imagine—

———ᏗᏗᏗ———

For years, I've wrestled with Steinbeck's ornery belief that a writer writes in utter loneliness trying to explain the inexplicable. I step off the mat and argue that ours is a crowded world of all the writers who came before us. But poke me in the dark blue night of the soul and I'll admit that we are laceratingly alone in trying get the silence to speak.

———ᏗᏗᏗ———

The postcard with the sleeping lion was postmarked
Tanzania. The signature read: Father Theodore Walters,
my college advisor, the man who taught me just what
Jesuitical really meant. It had been at least thirty years
since I had heard from him. "I received your books.
Thank the good Lord you are doing so well in your
career," he wrote in script. Then in bold print he wrote:
"But what you are doing for others?"

—⚏—

From the notebooks. Penedo, Portugal, 1991.
Rereading Alberto Manquel's *The Book of Reading* I
find some strange consolation in a seven-hundred-year-
old reflection, by Ibn Jima, a 13th century scholar, "The
student should always have with him an inkwell so as to
be able to write down things that he hears." If he could
faithfully carry an inkwell with him, I have no excuses
for going anywhere without pencil and notebook.
Stories are long distant races, aphorisms are sprints,
maxims a single step.

—⚏—

"When I worked for Matisse it was a harbor of peace,"
says the old French nun with the girlish smile,
remembering the sun-spangled afternoons when she
modeled for le maître, who described their flirtation as
a *floration*, a flowering of tenderness. Even the painter's
metaphors were colorful cut-outs.

—⚏—

Write not for book sales, reviews, money, or fame, but to find out who you are and how the world turns; write to live everything twice.

—⟋⟍—

Usually, the phrase *chilling words* is just a metaphor. Not for Shackleton and his crew. Out of character, but also nearly out of his mind, he confessed something that still has the frost hanging from every word. He confessed this to his first mate after their epic 720 nautical mile journey across the treacherous and icy Weddell Sea, then another 35 miles over the insanely dangerous mountain terrain of South Georgia Island, "I know that during the watch—it seemed to me often that we were four and not three." His mate responded, "Boss, I had a curious feeling that there was another person with us." The one that always walks beside us, as the mystics put it? Shackleton and his mate never dared explain themselves. After what they endured, they didn't have to.

—⟋⟍—

Your obligation as a writer is to speak the truth in such a way that it speaks to the truth of the reader. Otherwise, please don't feel obliged to write a word.

—⟋⟍—

Dive, delve, divine. Do not be satisfied with skating on surfaces. It's too easy to slip and slide away from the inky depths.

151

From the notebooks. Amsterdam, Netherlands, 1998. Why is Leonardo's lady smiling? What is in the letter that Vermeer's "Woman in Blue" is reading? What is so "wild" about Emily Dickinson's "wild nights"? What is so heartbreakingly beautiful about a Bach cello concerto? Why does the French actress Isabelle Hubert believe that acting has never taught her anything about herself? Why do I dream night after night of being woken up by buffalo-bellowing midnight freight trains running down the tracks near the house I grow up in? What was it that Saint Augustine smeared us with two thousand years go, that there is a special place in hell for those who ask too many questions. Why do I remember only that from seventh grade religion class?

—⚬⚬⚬—

The Sanskrit *ghbir* gave us our word *gift,* though it originally meant both give and receive, and it still does, or should, and that's my gift to you, if you'll take it and promise to pass it on.

—⚬⚬⚬—

Every time I hear the phrase "in its train," I hear Hank Williams' lonesome whippoorwill, and the harmonica moan of the night train, which just so happens to be the way I train my memory, so it moans.

—⚬⚬⚬—

Music, so as not to die of silence.

Music is proof of God. Bach, Mozart, Ella, Edith, Leonard, and Van wrote the scores that remind us of the need for musical metaphor, melodies to live by.

—∿—

Call it genius only if you can call it original.

—∿—

When words fail, music sails.

—∿—

Beauty is music for the eyes.

—∿—

Life goes on if someone sings the songs, dances the dances, tells the tales, and listens and sees and passes them on.

—∿—

Art, poetry, stories, music, drama, sports: matters of survival.

—∿—

I will never understand all the black ink pouring from God's pen. I don't trust anyone who says he does.

—∿—

Still, I listen; moved, I write.

My most stout resolutions have always been written in vanishing ink.

What happened to all the time when I wasn't writing? Where did all the time go when I was? It's time I find out.

If a juggler thinks about how many balls he has in the air, he drops one. If a hitter tries to think as the ball leaves the pitcher's hand, he swings and misses. If a writer thinks and types at the same time, the words drop, the meaning is missed. Write first, think later, then edit, then write again.

How cute, she cooed. *You want to be a writer.* Flipping her long blond hair back, she added, "But why do you have to take all those notes?" What could I say that wouldn't kill my chances with her that night? Bachelard's stinging words came to me, though I dared not risk sounding cute by saying them out loud: "In my heart there lodged a passion thorn. I tore it out one day and felt my heart no more." I left the thorn where it was supposed to be and counted myself twice as lucky.

Like the man almost said, Be kind to every one you meet because he or she could be an angel, a devil—or yourself in disguise.

—⟋⟍—

The truth of your life is closer to you than the vein thrombosing in your neck.

—⟋⟍—

Ever since the Cynics took Athens by storm, cynicism has been soul rust.

—⟋⟍—

Else your saying unsays it. Or else what? It's not what you say, it's how you say it. So say it well. Or else—

—⟋⟍—

Whenever I find a new writer, or painter, or singer, I feel like an astronomer discovering a new planet.

—⟋⟍—

The meandering river of language brings us happiness, which derives from hap, which gave us happen, meaning luck. Chances are, if we're lucky, happiness happens. If not, we are befallen by mishaps. And that's no typo.

—⟋⟍—

155

Another day studying everything, knowing nothing.

—◊—

If you want to be a wise guy, transform chance into fortune, fate into destiny, your lot in life into a lot of destiny. I'm sure I've said this before; I can't say it enough. I won't stop until I hear you say it.

—◊—

Conversation is impossible when everyone is talking. For the devious among us, communication is to be avoided at all costs.

—◊—

Augustine had it half right. I say, write and do what you will.

—◊—

A dictionary is a prism that reveals the rainbowing light of words, containing all the colors of the language, then dividing them into whirling kaleidoscopes of meaning.

—◊—

I took a speed reading class in college, which helped me get through *Ulysses* in one night. I think it was about some guy who got lost in Dublin.

PERSONIFCATIONS OF MUSIC AND GRAMMAR
PYTHAGORAS, TUNING A STRINGED INSTRUMENT,
AND DONATUS, AUTHOR OF *ARS GRAMMATICA*
ROYAL PORTAL, CHARTRES CATHEDRAL, FRANCE, 1987
PHOTOGRAPHY BY PHIL COUSINEAU

Nowadays everyone wants to write a book and few
want to read one, unless it's theirs. I long for thenadays
when we wanted to read each other.

—⟋⟍—

Contact with the sacred is not a luxury or an indulgence,
but a deep necessity—for the soul, anyway, if you know
to contact it.

—⟋⟍—

If you do not bring forth your genius, your genius will
wither and destroy your imagination.

—⟋⟍—

Let's forget it never happened, she cooed, and remember
not to start over.

—⟋⟍—

Sometimes silence is the best revenge; always revenge is
best silenced.

—⟋⟍—

Genius conjures serious play at will.

—⟋⟍—

Those who build castles in the air must learn to walk
on clouds.

Don't bother unless you enjoy being disturbed.

—⟋⟍—

A book is a mirror with a memory.

—⟋⟍—

What chiseling is to sculpture, reading is to the soul.

—⟋⟍—

Whatever spurs you to action reads your mind before you've thought of it.

—⟋⟍—

There is no lost-and-found department for time.

—⟋⟍—

Reading proofs usually proves more about the editor than the writer.

—⟋⟍—

To be proud of not having read a book since you got out of school is to remain a child, without the curiosity.

—⟋⟍—

Those who build castles in the air must build imaginary drawbridges.

The real work. Audaciousness begins it, tenaciousness ends it. Or it's not bodacious.

—ɯ—

An aphorism is oratory run through a condensery.

—ɯ—

Scritch. The clawing sound coming from the other side of the wall as you try to sleep. Rhymes with *eldritch.* Something is licking its chops, trying to get in. *Scritch.* You stare at the door handle and feel stupid as dirt, not knowing if you let it in or let it out. Eerie how scritch rhymes with eldritch.

—ɯ—

From my Book of Questions: After all the folderol, all the dithering, your creative life comes down to this bone-breaker: *What were you waiting for?*

—ɯ—

And then I saw myself in the circus mirror for what I really was, twisting in my own reflection in utter disbelief of what I have become—

—ɯ—

Whatever I can't get out of my head should stay there. Friends shout, "Change the channel!" I tell them it's just a brain sprain.

The worst thing someone can say about you is that you are soulless; the best that you are soulful. No definition of theology required. Just drop a dime in the diner jukebox and play a little Motown, if you need a boost.

—◊—

Be careful who you share your proudest achievements with: twenty percent of your friends and family will be jealous and the other eighty will wish you'd never been born.

—◊—

From the notebooks. Tea with Robert Thurman, American Buddhist scholar. Stay off the edge of the abyss – or learn to fly, he says, leaning in. Only way to learn? Your daily practice is evaluating your daily moments. Christ, what did I miss while I was taking notes. His one marble eye that never moved; the other one that never needed to.

—◊—

Grazing in the mystery. Chewing the cud of aphorisms.

—◊—

Surely, there is no greater wisdom than kindness.

—◊—

I have half a mind to tell you what's on the other half.

—◊—

Unlike many, I never dreamed of a life of making money, only a life of making marvels, books, films, radio and TV shows. Art-making. Nor the Life of Reilly, the Life of Marvels.

—◊—

I write to justify being born, which I find otherwise impossible to justify.

—◊—

Writing is like a woodcutter making a path through the forest—

—◊—

Life's a pitch—then you die on third.

—◊—

And there are moments—the susussurus of my son's breathing in my arms when he was an infant, the languorous chase of a Golden Retriever after a tossed ball along the bay, the soughing last words of Cyrano de Bergerac—that prevent me from lamenting over my writing millions of words that have not yet compensated for the inadequate reach of my language.

162

Agon. Ancient Greek for contest in athletics, art, horse racing, theater, any competition. Startling but illuminating that it is the root of our own agony.

—⁓—

Sports, n. From the Old Italian *desporto*, to carry away, the root of transport, which is what happens to competitive athletes, audiences, and television executives. We get carried away trying to get carried away.

—⁓—

It's sporting of the gods that sports don't build character as much as reveal it.

—⁓—

He who was born on third and thinks he hit a triple will be thrown out trying to steal home.

—⁓—

The ideal ballgame is one you would watch even if you never caught the final score.

—⁓—

You can't win 'em all, but you can learn to live with the losses.

—⁓—

All art is the search for the deeply real, so is science and religion, travel, sports. Everything is unreal until experienced otherwise, or surreal if we never learn to describe it.

—⟪⟫—

The beginning of the end is not the end and is not the beginning either. That's why we keep score.

—⟪⟫—

Where did it all begin, with the stick or the ball?

—⟪⟫—

The greatest athletes, like the finest storytellers, and the most mesmerizing actors, have the uncanny ability to slow life down, the capacity to create the illusion of stopping it altogether, which is why we remember those games, stories, and plays as timeless.

—⟪⟫—

When the storm began, Noah was hoping for a rain out.

—⟪⟫—

Every baseball game is an odyssey, the long and circuitous journey past gods and monsters who want to distract and delay you on the path, who challenge your desire to get home again.

Baseball, n. At the last night game ever played at Tiger Stadium, I quietly pulled out of my wallet my Topps '62 Al Kaline baseball card, and when I was sure no one was watching I used a pencil to write as faintly as possible the kind of epiphany that come to a fan out in the bleachers watching the team he's loved all his life: *Baseball is a pitching machine that throws metaphors.* Whew, now that I've written it here I can finally erase those pencil marks and put the card back in my wallet.

—⦚—

"Trust the grind," I heard the grizzled ballplayer tell the sportswriter, who showed him his ink-stained fingertips

—⦚—

Baseball is to football as chess is to Russian roulette.

—⦚—

"Pop," my son asked me when he was five. "Did you know that baseball is in the Bible?" Playing along, I looked shocked, "No, for heaven's sake, Jack. I didn't know that! Where?" His giggle made my heart somersault, "*Sheesh, Pop, in the big inning.* Get it? Beginning, big inning?" I'll die a happy man if he inherited nothing else from me except my goofy love of word play.

—⦚—

Something in the invisible world is making we don't
know what, which must be why a baseball curves the
way it does.

—⟋⟍⟍—

You can't hit what you can't see, but you can't see what
you weren't expecting.

—⟋⟍⟍—

Whoever plays catch catches the give-and-take
of friendship.

—⟋⟍⟍—

The truest search is the search to be sure we know what
we think we know.

—⟋⟍⟍—

If you're not living on the edge, you're dying in
the cracks, and taking up too much room.

—⟋⟍⟍—

The clever ones among us never let you know they
know it.

—⟋⟍⟍—

THE PERSONIFICATION OF THE ATHLETIC STRUGGLE
OLYMPIC HISTORY EXHIBITION
NATIONAL ARCHAEOLOGICAL MUSEUM OF ATHENS, 2004.
PHOTOGRAPHY BY PHIL COUSINEAU.

Inspired by one of my literary heroes, Raymond Chandler, I keep obsessive lists of character names for future stories. High on my list is *Lefty Eldritch*, a faintly sinister name I plan to use in my baseball novel about a screwball pitcher with a big heart. Sonicky names are easier to visualize and remember. Who can forget Cannonball Titcomb, Johnny Dickshot, Bud Weiser, Lil Stoner, Mysterious Walker, Three-Finger Brown, Moonlight Graham, King Lear, King Kelly, Chief Sockalexis, Phenomenal Smith, or Charlie "Paw Paw" Maxwell? Name games. Why writers love baseball more than any other sport. We know we don't know a thing until we name it. If you don't believe me, as Casey said, "You can look it up."

—⚬—

North Beach, spring, 1997. Wake up in middle of night thinking *I'm living on loose change*. I've learned from the polyfabulous James Hillman that the one place to take puns seriously is in dreams. *Change, change.* I rise and walk down the hall into the living room where she is nursing our son. *Change, change.* All has changed—but me, I'm thinking. I had to pull coins—*loose change*—from out of the couch cushions today to pay for my baby boy's medicine. *Change. Coins. Pocket change.* Change or be changed. So which dream pun do I believe? Change, or stay loose?

—⚬—

Theory, smeary. The only thing I'm looking for any more in art is a glimmer of the writer or artist or singer's ferocious need that couldn't be satisfied anywhere else, that found no respite except in their art. All the rest, as D. H. L. said, is *persiflage*.

—⟋⟋⟋⟋—

Sharing a story with someone is like the nineteenth-century practice of keeping a stereopticon in the parlor to offer a guest a view of unknown worlds. Our story is the other lens that gives our listeners binocular vision.

—⟋⟋⟋⟋—

"Try kindness, try to be a little kinder." Aldous Huxley's advice to my friend Huston, who passed it on to me on stage at UCLA with such tenderness in his voice I felt Huxley's presence for one fugacious moment. "He told me that it was embarrassing to have studied the human condition his entire life and was only able to come up with that for a conclusion." Sometimes one moment is enough to last a lifetime, then somebody else's lifetime, if you tell it right.

—⟋⟋⟋⟋—

Wandering through life without trying to glean some meaning is like roaming through a magnificent library without tilting your head to read the spines, or worse, without reading a book.

169

No story without metamorphosis. No change, no story.
Nothing worth talking about.

—⟋⟍—

Beyond the pale of wondrous special effects, shock cut
editing, or gasp-grasping cinematography, explosive
Method acting, the most amazing thing to see in a movie
is simply this: *the uncanny capacity of an actor to
express a new thought moving through her mind that
she allows us to see passing across her face.*

—⟋⟍—

Live for the chase with the hell-hounds for the
unachievable meaning of the world, the hunt for the
deeply real, it being just enough to give you a ferocious
sense of purpose.

—⟋⟍—

Dreaming of a half-timbered country pub in the Scottish
Highlands. Shriveling in embarrassment. Turning to a
mate at the pub. I'm saying, "Oh my Lord, I just had a
sip of your finest Laphroaig whiskey and never noticed
it going down. How was yours?" Once again, waking up
drenched in the cold sweat of the unlived life.

—⟋⟍—

Loving her was like being hugged by the arms of the
Venus de Milo.

I write jagged stories, ragged poems, barbed maxims, and twisted aphorisms not to appear any wiser than I am, but to honor the broken parts of my life. That's why I have caulk in my pen and spackle to patch my manuscripts filled with the necessary fragments.

— ⁂ —

Perspective, I'm always looking for perspective. Today I found it in Attenborough's new *Nature* series, hearing him intone how humans are small and insignificant enough to swim through the man-sized blood vessels of a blue whale. Perspective. There's no understanding without it.

— ⁂ —

Overheard in a Birmingham, Alabama catfish restaurant, 1993. You're one two-timer too many, she done said, and I done said back to her you're living in the past and she done came back to me and said that just proves we ain't got no future.

— ⁂ —

Eavesdropping in a Delta diner, a young girl with a fire-engine-red cheeks sighing to her parents as she sat down with a *whoosh* of relief, "My feet are smiling."

— ⁂ —

Like believing you have a chance with the cute-as-a-
calico-kitten waitress in the all-night diner who calls
you, "Hon'."

—⁓—

He went all orthogonal on me,
she said, a tangential thing
said from a perpendicular angle.

—⁓—

Love, a steamy encounter with desire.

—⁓—

A man's desire is testicular and perpendicular;
a woman's, horizontal and orthogonal.
It's a miracle that we ever find one another.

—⁓—

Falling in love is no proof of gravitation, but it does take
your breath away when you feel the paratrooper's
ground rush as you fall into your lover's arms.

—⁓—

I must have heard Dion DiMucci's doo-wopping,
sax-walloping, finger-snapping "Runaround Sue" about
a million times, but mumbled my way through the lyrics
when I sang along. I never realized Dion must have been

one of our, *ahem*, wisdom keepers, not till tonight when his growling chorus finally rang clear: "*So, people, let me put you wise,* Sue goes out with other guys... *Whooaaaa—doooo-wop-wop.*" I get it now—*singing* your heart out is what makes us wise. *Whooaaaa—doooo-wop-wop....whooaaa!*

———∭———

Couldn't help myself from jotting it down after hearing my beehive-haired waitress, in a South Carolina bar, circa 1986. She even gave me the pencil she'd hidden in her hair. "Darlin'," she drawled, "he done spun my heart around like a centrifuge." Language oughta done spin us around like that all the darn time.

———∭———

Flirty, she said, breezily, "Sorry if I've been flirty." Smiling, he saw in his mind's eye an image of the old word's Dutch origins, a bee flitting from flower to flower, in search of—and the word came to him. "Honey," he thought, but he didn't dare say it. Instead, out came, "What a sweet thing to say." Some things are better left breezily unsaid.

———∭———

The first time we met your words reached me like a message whishing around a whispering gallery. If I listen closely, I can still feel your breath in my ear.

173

Unfinished story from the notebooks. April 1996. One bedazzled day as a boy I watched a stampede of thunderclouds, wave after angry wave, as turbulent as the gnarled hands of a storm god, fuming over the sandlot where I was playing the third ballgame of that endless summer day. I've never written about it because I never knew how to describe those clouds. Even after consulting my hand-size *Golden Book of Clouds*. How do we describe what we don't have a name for? Two years ago, I learned of the Cloud Appreciation Society because it had just announced its first new cloud classification in over fifty years: "Undulatus Asperatus." Fifty years after the sighting, I finally had a name for that undulating, mad, melting meringue of clouds that canceled our ballgame. We were leading 43-42 when the rains came. I was standing at the plate. The bases were loaded—

—ᨏᨏ—

Recognizing a curious cloud shape does not make it a spaceship from outer space, no more than *not* recognizing the shape of another religion's god descending from the heavens to save a strange group of believers doesn't make them infidels.

—ᨏᨏ—

It's impossible to see something for what it is until we have a word for it.

And then dusk dropped a vermilion ribbon over the evening dusted olive grove and brushed the silver-maned windmill, while the moon wore a serene green crown, and the sea became tinted with Greek mystery. And then it was time to get back to work.

—⚬—

Aphorism, n. A rhapsody on the theme of the long desire to see clearly and deeply to new horizons of perception, as revealed by its loamy roots in the Greek *aphorizein*, "To define, mark off or determine." If that sounds familiar, that is because it gave us *horizon* and *boundary*. Hippocrates must have had this in mind when he coined the word *Aphorismi* for his first collection of sayings, which stretched the boundaries of healing words beyond the known world. I'll take an oath on it.

—⚬—

It's not how you tripped over the cobblestones, it's how you got back on your feet.

—⚬—

The creative work we long for is achieved by love, beauty, and imagination, mostly love. And we wonder why we often feel a frisson of the erotic. If we don't, it ain't art.

—⚬—

The one and only story is how things change—or don't. Writing is not a record of a struggle to find hope but the traces of the effort to *make* it.

—∿—

I want you to say of me when I'm gone that he was a man who crested the hill, singing as he was writing.

—∿—

Writing was my way of allowing myself to dream on paper; a guy's got to dream.

—∿—

What matters is not beginning the work but seeing it through to the end.

—∿—

Not all who look, see. Not all who see, understand. Not at all.

—∿—

If you don't love your work, it won't work.

—∿—

The book is longer than I anticipated because I didn't have the luxury of endless time to make it shorter.

Contrariwise, experience is what happens to you,
wisdom is what you learned from what happened.
So wise up.

—m—

We can be whatever we want, but we can't want
whatever we want.

—m—

You can never get enough of what you really don't need.
So quit asking.

—m—

It behooves you to get a horse that isn't lame.

—m—

Don't wait till you're hungry to plant your garden.

—m—

To err is human; to forgive yourself, divine.

—m—

If I were to riff on saxophonist Charlie Parker's lyrical
affirmation of music, I would say that you can whittle
down the meaning of why I write to: *Yes, yes, yes ... no,
yes, yes ... no, no, yes, yes ... yes ...*

—m—

If wisdom begins in wonder, where does it end?

177

UNDULATUS ASPERATUS, CLOUDS
BIG SUR, CALIFORNIA, 2014

Condense, compress. Tell me your troubles, tell me everything. In a word or two, no more than a phrase. Tell me everything.

—◊◊◊—

In no time at all, now will be a long time ago.

—◊◊◊—

I will spend time with you only if you know secret things, otherwise I'd rather be alone.

—◊◊◊—

That epitaph painted on the cross stuck onto the gunslinger's grave in Tombstone, Arizona: "Be what you is cuz if you be what you ain't then you ain't what you is." Ain't that just the way it's always been, at least at the bittersweet end?

—◊◊◊—

A life of contribution: the finest masterpiece.

—◊◊◊—

"*Ah*, a real conversation," the hunchback camel driver told me one blistering afternoon in the Sinai. "Now that is the real Garden of Eden."

—◊◊◊—

The two worlds are separated by a single story.

Too many words; too little wisdom.

—ɷ—

I know next to nothing. I wonder what's next.

—ɷ—

Awakening is labyrinthine.

—ɷ—

Opening the journal, in I strode—

—ɷ—

Hope glides, resignation recoils.

—ɷ—

And give me this day my daily wonder.

—ɷ—

Her smile was her most beautiful curve.

—ɷ—

An aphorism: the shortest way to go long and deep.

—ɷ—

Silence is golden; conversation goldener.

"Mama, mama, I was whirled without end," muttered the boy, dizzy from the rollercoaster. "Amen," sighed his mother. "Amen."

—⁓—

Funny how serendipity works best when we work the most.

—⁓—

Expect nothing, be surprised by everything.

—⁓—

To the naked eye, deep space looks cold, dark, empty, soulless. And yet, and yet, and yet …

—⁓—

When I asked the Connemara farmer how far the old dirt road went, he doffed his plaid cap, scratched his bewhiskered chin, and said in a bog-deep brogue, "To the end, lad, to the end."

—⁓—

How soon later becomes never.

—⁓—

At night I walk next to myself, wondering why.

—⁓—

181

Writing to make you feel something, else my writing
unwrites it.

—ᵐ—

By all means, hitch your wagon to a star but don't forget
to water your horses.

—ᵐ—

And pages to go before I sleep, pages and pages to go
before I sleep.

—ᵐ—

A good day's writing is the night's best pillow.

—ᵐ—

Writing is the astrolabe for my never-ending odyssey.

—ᵐ—

Like the Armenian sculptor who carved a red-capped
baseball player out of a grain rice I am a miniaturist, but
with words.

—ᵐ—

Promise me, you whispered on our first night together,
the last word you say to me every night
will always be
love.

Tintagel Castle
King Arthur's Birthplace
Cornwall, England, 2016
Photography by Phil Cousineau

IN LIEU OF AN EPILOGUE

"Writing a book ages a man. The day comes when a conclusion has to be reached, time to finish up. One sees what one's first experiments came to. All throughout life one has written books to keep up the habit of writing, in the belief that outside of one's thinking remained free, that one's destiny lay outside of writing."

—Gaston Bachelard, *The Poetics of Fire*

ACKNOWLEDGMENTS

In the spirit of aphoristic writing I would like to express my pithiest thanks to those who have been kind and patient enough to make the time to read the various editions of this manuscript over the last ten years. Those doughty readers include Willis Barnstone, James Norwood Pratt, Mort Rosenblum, Michael Grosso, Robert A. Johnson, Valerie Andrews, Chris Franek, Lou Ann Granger, Fr. Gary Young, John Borton, April Bosshard, and Joanne Warfield. Special thanks to the late Angeles Arrien, Alexander Eliot, and Huston Smith, all of whom were gracious enough to read early rough drafts of the manuscript and were unstinting in their support and encouragement for me to carry on.

For someone like me, who does not live by words alone, I want to bow and doff my hat, like the Aran Fisherman I met on the Aran Islands, to a handful of singers, songwriters, and composers whose music kept me going. Ten years ago, it was Mozart's buoyant piano concertos that helped launch the book. Along the long and winding road there was Van the Man and Leonard Cohen and the pride of Knoxville, RB Morris. Over the last few months, I discovered the brilliant blues singer and guitar player Sue Foley, whose incantatory albums and videos helped me to "bring it on home." And then there is my fellow Detroiter, poet Philip Levine, who has been a constant source of not just inspiration but *goading* because reading him reminds me of the god's call for us to be as original and audacious as possible.

Finally, I am profoundly indebted to the polymath Stuart Balcomb, for his celestial music, which was another soundtrack for the composition of this book, and for his gifts of wise counsel and lynx-eyed copy editing, which rescued the manuscript from purblind grammatical errors. You showed me that the glorious comma is more than a period with a tail; it can be as beautiful as a note in a musical score. All told, everyone's encouragement over the passel of years moves through this manuscript like the moon-driven tide. For the book design, which is an art form in itself, I am grateful to Jim Shubin, the Book Alchemist, in Novato, California, for turning the lead of ordinary pages and files into the gold of a finished book. His creation of the elegant book cover and the classy interior has been a tremendous gift for this project. Thanks, also, to Ingram Spark, in Berkeley, California for the printing of the book, and to my friends at Café 901 Columbus, in North Beach, for keeping my table available …

A final flourish of thanks to my family, Jo and Jack Cousineau, for their love and patience, and their willingness to live in a House on a Hill made of Books and Love.

ABOUT THE AUTHOR

There was a young aphorist from Detroit
Who drove through dictionaries like A. J. Foyt
He strove for breviloquence
In an age of magniloquence,
Until he was laconically adroit.

PHIL COUSINEAU is a writer, photographer, filmmaker,storyteller, lecturer, writing and creativity consultant, anthologist, quotologist, and an accidental aphorist. He has published more than 40 nonfiction books, earned over 20 documentary film scriptwriting credits, and contributed to over 50 other books. His work has been won dozens of international awards, and nominated for many awards, including an Academy Award and an Emmy Award. As a travel leader, he has led art and literary tours all over the world. Currently, Cousineau is co-writer and host of Global Spirit, which plays nationwide on PBS and Link TV and streams around the world at: https://www.linktv.org/shows/global-spirit.

He is guest host on New Dimensions Radio, the longest continuous-running radio interview show in history. Cousineau is a Fellow of the Joseph Campbell Foundation, a member of the Board of Directors of Sacred Sites International, and is one of the founding mentors of the Paths to Publishing Program at Book Passage, in Corte Madera, California. Cousineau lives with his family on Telegraph Hill in word-mad North Beach, San Francisco, California.

COLOPHON

The Accidental Aphorist was designed by Phil Cousineau and Jim Shubin, The Book Alchemist, in Marin County, California. The title was typeset in American Typewriter, which is a slab serif typeface created in 1974 by Joel Kaden and Tony Stan for International Typeface Corporation. The body text was set in Sabon designed by Jan Tschichold, a Leipzig-born typographer in the 1960s. Sabon took its name from Jacques Sabon, who issued the first-known type specimen book in the sixteenth century.

This book is printed in a first edition of 1000 copies.

For more copies of The Accidental Aphorist or other Sisyphus Press titles, or any other Phil Cousineau books, films, postcards, letterpress broadsides, television shows, or radio shows please contact:

 Sisyphus Press
P. O. Box 330098
San Francisco, CA 94133

pilgrimage@earthlink.net

Further information about the author's writing consultations or art and literary tours is available on his website: www.philcousineau.com

N. B.: No dictionaries, no encyclopedias, nor gnomes were harmed in the making of this book.

CPSIA information can be obtained
at www.ICGtesting.com
Printed in the USA
FSOW03n0337170317
31760FS